HOW LONG, O LORD, HOW LONG?

DEVOTIONS *for the* UNEMPLOYED *and* THOSE WHO LOVE THEM

Unexpected unemployment is an incredibly difficult experience. Thankfully, Dale Kreienkamp has provided an honest, faith-filled, clear devotional on how not only to weather this storm, but to come through it even stronger than you entered it. If you're between jobs or know someone who is, read it.

John O'Leary
International Speaker, Podcast host and
#1 National Best-Selling Author of *On Fire*

Work has been an integral part of nearly my entire life of 75 years. As a young child I did chores at home. During elementary school, high school, college, and seminary, I always had a part time job. But then, after 48 years of full time professional church work, including seven triennial elections to regional and national ecclesiastical leadership, I was unelected. Terminated. Someone else was elected to the position I had held for nine long and hard but meaningful and fulfilling years. Although my period of unemployment was brief, I experienced all the emotions and challenges described by my friend Dale Kreienkamp. Some of those emotions still exist today. How I wish I had been blessed back then, eight years ago, with Dale's 80 Devotions for the Unemployed. His experience, suggestions, advice, and counsel are laced with poignant scripture references that provide help, healing, and hope for the unemployed. Whatever the time or reason for your season of unemployment, you'll be blessed by *How Long, Oh Lord, How Long?*, even as I have been, eight years after the fact.

Dr. Gerald B. Kieschnick
President Emeritus, The Lutheran Church—Missouri Synod
and Chief Executive Officer, Legacy Deo

This collection of devotions captures the real emotions, struggles and discoveries of being unemployed. In and through these emotions, questions, doubts, and fears shared, he weaves threads of hope in the midst of this journey with powerful Words from Scripture. Each of the 80 devotions brings refreshment, honesty, new perspectives, and an "ah ha" surprise from God for the unemployed, their families, and friends.

Lee Hovel
retired pastor and friend

I have found Dale's book to be a tremendous resource for providing insights into the struggles of the unemployed as well as support and wisdom for themselves and their families! The book has proven to be a very powerful aid to help them to navigate the ups and downs while searching for employment.

Sally Gafford, Ph.D., LMFT, LPC, NBCC, AAMFT
Marriage and Family Therapy Therapist

How Long, O Lord, How Long? is insightful, practical, and filled with the rich life experiences of a disciple of Jesus. In Samaritan language, Dale's heart for helping those who have been left beat up on the side of the road can be experienced on every page. The journey of job loss and employment search should not be taken without these helpful chapters.

Rev. Thomas M. Gundermann
University Pastor, Concordia, Saint Paul

His experience on both sides of the conversation makes Dale Kreienkamp the ideal Christian to offer keen spiritual insight into the journey through unemployment.

Rev. Dr. Scott K. Seidler
Senior Pastor, Concordia Lutheran Church

A powerful heart testimony of someone who is unemployed for those who have become unemployed—What is God saying? What does it mean? What does it mean for me in my life NOW?

Walter M. Schoedel
retired teacher, pastor, administrator, editor, counselor, innovator

HOW LONG, O LORD, HOW LONG?

DEVOTIONS *for the* UNEMPLOYED *and* THOSE WHO LOVE THEM

DALE KREIENKAMP

TENTH
POWER

Elgin, IL · Tyler, TX

TENTHPOWERPUBLISHING
www.tenthpowerpublishing.com

Design by Inkwell Creative.

Softcover 978-1-938840-20-3
e-book 978-1-938840-21-0
10 9 8 7 6 5 4 3 2 1

INTRODUCTION

It was the best of times, it was the worst of times… The opening line of Charles Dickens' novel *A Tale of Two Cities* is very appropriate for the journey of unemployment. If you are reading this book, you (or someone you know) has lost their job, which is the beginning of an amazing journey. When the journey is complete it's possible to look back and remember some of the most wonderful moments of joy in your life, truly the "best of times." But you will also remember heartaches along the way, which, in looking back, won't seem as significant as they did "in the moment." I can tell you from personal experience, when you are "in the moment" of heartache, it can feel overwhelming, "the worst of times." The good news is the joy in this journey can far outweigh the heartache.

If you aren't currently experiencing unemployment, but your spouse or someone you care about is, this book will help you understand what's going on in their life. It will give you a glimpse into their world, the many emotions, challenges, and heartaches they will experience. You'll be able to take a little "walk in their shoes" with them. With a better understanding, you will be a better support for them.

In today's world, being unemployed isn't uncommon and probably represents more of a "norm" for workers, as organizations often choose to shed the "expense" of employees and their salaries to meet a goal, meet the bottom line target, or to be more efficient. While it's not uncommon, it isn't something people talk about; they just silently hope being unemployed doesn't happen to them.

The loss of a job is a major life event, and it shouldn't be underestimated. Look at any list of the most stressful life events and you will surely find "loss of a job" ranked high. Why? For most of us the connection to a job is twofold: 1) It is another "community" of people we are connected to and work with, full of close personal relationships where we often spend more hours than we do with our family. 2) For many of us, our "identity" is tied up in what we do for a living.

The good news is that your period of unemployment, no matter how long it lasts, **will end**. You will find something new or begin to do something different; the questions are *what*, *where*, and *when*. In fact, God already knows what he has in store for you. He wants us to go through this process, to rely on him, to draw us closer to him. The good news is when we get there, it will be awesome and full of joy. But while you are waiting for it to end, you may often utter the cry I did, the same cry of the psalmist David long before us: *My soul is in anguish. How long, O Lord, how long?* (Psalm 6:3).

MY STORY

Most of us don't spend much time thinking about the loss of a job. You know it can happen, but you don't expect it yourself. I've been through this process twice in my life, once after working 25 years for the same organization and once after 10 years. Both times I was fully committed to my place of work, sacrificing my personal life and time with family and friends, all for the sake of doing my job well and advancing the mission of the organization. I was good at what I did too, but in the end, it didn't matter how good I was at my job.

My profession has been as a human resources executive. Because of my background, I already knew some things about the process of employment (finding jobs), but I received a "master's degree in life" during my first period of unemployment. It was then that I first began to draft many of these devotions, but I moved on and the drafts stayed on the shelf.

Then, 15 years later, it happened again to me, and I earned my "Ph.D." on the subject. It was during this time that I knew God wanted me to finish this work to help others who were going through the same experience. These experiences gave me a new perspective, brought me even closer to my wife, my children and my good friends, all whom were a source of strength, love and support throughout my unemployment.

During my periods of unemployment, I never liked telling people I was "out of work," "between jobs," or "in transition"— all phrases that get used often. I preferred to tell people I was on *sabbatical,* which is a break from your work, a period of rest that might last from a couple of months to a year. As I look back, that's what I needed, and I believe you too might need one now. During your "sabbatical" you are in for an emotional journey of "ups" and "downs." It's a ride that no one can really prepare you for; you will just have to experience it.

I've shared the same two thoughts with many people when talking about this experience. I wouldn't wish the experience on anyone because it is a tough time. *But* I wouldn't trade the experience for anything, because it made me a better person, one who has learned to give more of my life over to God, to trust him. At many times during this process, you'll feel all alone. But you are not alone; *God is with you*, even though at times you may wonder if he's there.

WHAT IS THIS BOOK?

In my time off, I found there are many books available about how to deal with death, divorce, illness, but not much out there on how Christians deal with unemployment. I decided to write this book to help others who are experiencing this same challenge in their own life, or indirectly as the loved one or friend of someone unemployed. As a Christian, I lean heavily upon God, knowing he is with me and that he will work something good in what I find challenging. It is my prayer that the same might happen for you. While I'm not a theologian, I have added Scripture verses and my thoughts about their application in this journey.

Each chapter will cover some of the emotions often felt by those who are unemployed and some biblical insights to help you in dealing with these emotions. All scripture reflects the NIV translation, unless I've noted otherwise. You'll feel many of these emotions regardless of whether you were the head of a corporation or one of the lowest-paid staff members where you worked. Your emotional makeup, or ability to deal with unemployment, isn't related in any way to how much money you make. Some devotions will be more meaningful to you than others because we are all different. Many you will go back to over and over again in dealing with the emotions and issues of this journey. I went back to my own work many times.

If you are married or you are in a significant relationship with someone, I encourage both of you to read this. Read it together and talk about it. This is a shared experience and understanding what's happening to the one you love is important.

God allows us experiences that are often challenging and not much fun, in order to strengthen us. He then asks that we help others who are in a similar position. I hope that if you read this book and we ever meet, you'll be able to tell me about someone you helped because of your own experience.

ORGANIZATION OF THE DEVOTIONS

Organizing the book was a challenge, recognizing that we all come to different places in the journey at a different time. I chose to organize these devotions in way that is consistent with the "change curve," which followed what I experienced. What is the "change curve"? It's a model to help you understand the stages of transition a person goes through in dealing with a personal or organizational change. If you aren't familiar, see Appendix A.

Topical Index

Recognizing that everyone who reads this book will read at their own pace and their emotions will be different, I've included a topical index in Appendix B. If you are struggling with a particular emotion or issue, the topical index will highlight relevant devotions, allowing you to get the support you need when you need it.

Books Worth Reading

Appendix C is a list of books worth reading during your journey, some related to life, some related to a job search. Many of them are referenced in these devotions.

Sample Communications

Appendix D contains communication samples I used during my search.

Interview Preparation

Appendix E has some tips on preparing for an interview.

I pray for God's richest blessings for you and your loved ones in your journey.

Dale Kreienkamp

TABLE OF CONTENTS

DEDICATION

I AM INDEBTED TO my wife, Deb, the love of my life, who is my biggest supporter and cheerleader. I could not have gone through this journey (twice) without her at my side.

I'm thankful for the support of our three sons and their wives, Dan and Jen, Don and Amanda, Drew and Charli. They continued to love and care for me, deepening an already awesome relationship.

I also am thankful for my grandchildren, Arthur, Isaiah, Noah, and Andi, who all kept me from getting too serious about anything and didn't notice any difference in me because they only knew me as Grandpa. The love of children and grandchildren can help anyone through tough times.

I'm also thankful for my family and the many good friends who cared, encouraged and supported me through my journey. Your phone calls, emails, and opportunities to get together to talk were invaluable to me. To those who opened their schedule to meet with me when I asked for their time, many who didn't know me, I say "thanks." Please know that I will repay your kindness and pay it forward in meeting with others as you met me.

Finally, I am forever indebted to Jane Wilke, my good friend and editor. She's made my writing better for many years and this book wouldn't have happened without her gifts.

KEY TO TOPICS

 ANGER/LETTING GO

 ANXIETY, FEAR & WORRY

 DESPAIR

 **JOB SEARCH**

 **OTHER INSIGHTS**

 RE-DIRECTION

 SELF CONFIDENCE

 USE OF TIME

 WAITING

 WHY

THIS IS YOUR RACE

HAVE YOU EVER RUN in a race? I've participated in a few of them in my life. In a race, everyone who is participating has the same goal (to win) and the conditions and the course are the same. But life is a different kind of race.

In the book of Hebrews, the Apostle Paul points out that our life is our own and it is unique to us. *Therefore, since we are surrounded by such a great cloud of witnesses, let us throw off everything that hinders and the sin that so easily entangles. And let us run with perseverance **the race marked out for us**, fixing our eyes on Jesus, the pioneer and perfecter of faith. For the joy set before him he endured the cross, scorning its shame, and sat down at the right hand of the throne of God* (Hebrews 12:1-2).

You can compare your life with that of anyone else, but it's not the same. From the day you were born, your life has been different from every other person who ever lived on this earth. There is only one "you," created by God for his purpose. You've had different parents, grandparents, siblings, and friends. I can easily go on and on regarding how unique you are, but what I really want you to know is that the race you are now running—your period of unemployment—is unique to you; it's yours alone.

While there are many people who are or have been or even

will be unemployed, they aren't "you." The danger, especially in difficult or stressful times, is in comparing our situation to that of someone else's. For example, you may know of someone who found a job in three months while you remain unemployed at four months. If you dwell on the comparison, it will only add more stress that you don't need.

The other challenge you'll face is the advice others will want to give. You'll hear things like "you should be doing ___," "don't do ___," "that's a bad industry to be in, avoid it," "when I was looking I did ___," and so on. Everyone means well, but the advice of others may or may not help you. Hear me on this: Be a good listener, as there may be some wisdom in what they say, but ultimately, you'll need to pray about it, weigh what they have to say, then do what you believe is right for you. And then don't second-guess yourself.

In verse 2 of Hebrews 12, the Apostle Paul gives important direction on what we should be doing every day, but especially on this journey: "fixing our eyes on Jesus." As you move forward, look to Jesus for direction. You won't know what path to follow if you don't look to him.

Your life may be changing, but God isn't. He's there to love you and help you through the changes along this journey.

I CAN'T BELIEVE THIS HAPPENED TO ME

I CAN'T BELIEVE THIS happened to me. It's doesn't seem real, but it is. It's like living a bad dream. I no longer have a job and it wasn't a decision I made on my own. Maybe it's the same for you. I had a good job and I was good at it. Was I perfect? No, far from it, but I was very good at what I did for a living. In fact, before my position was eliminated, I had numerous successes that benefited the organization in many ways. How could this happen to me?

When given the news, I was shocked and stunned. I couldn't believe what I had just heard. One minute I'm employed, the next my world has been turned upside down. How about you? Were you surprised like me, or had you seen it coming? Either way, it hurts when reality sets in. Being in shock is normal, that feeling where you want to wake up and discover it was all a bad dream. For a while, *nothing* will seem normal. How long you remain in shock will be different for everyone and I urge you, do not to rush it. Nature must take its course.

The flood of thoughts and emotions you'll face next may vary depending on your personal situation, but they might include any (or all) of these:

- I'm relieved it's over.
- I'm angry.
- Why did this happen; what did I do?
- Why not someone else?
- How will I tell my spouse?
- What will I say to my children?

- What will others think?
- How will we make it financially?
- Will I ever find another job?
- What will I say to my coworkers?
- What will I say to those who worked for me?
- I'm afraid.

Through it all, God wants you to give those emotions and concerns over to him. In Psalm 50:15 we read *Call on me in the day of trouble; I will deliver you, and you will honor me.* God knows what you are going through and I want you to know that, no matter how unnerved or frightened you might be, he won't leave you, ever!

Be strong and courageous. Do not be afraid or terrified because of them, for the Lord your God goes with you; he will never leave you nor forsake you (Deuteronomy 31: 6). God spoke these words to Joshua as he prepared to lead God's children into the promised land. I have no doubt that Joshua was anxious; he was a new leader and they faced huge challenges. But God told him what he also says to us: Put your big boy/girl pants on because this won't be easy. But don't be afraid; I'm with you and we'll get through this together.

Rest in the knowledge that God is present. He is with you every day, both the good days and the difficult days.

WHY?

WHY DID THIS HAPPEN? That's something I'm sure you'd like to know. You may have been given a reason, but that doesn't necessarily answer the question deep-down inside of you. Most of us want to know what we did to lose our job or what we could have done differently to keep it. I certainly did.

Something I'm guilty of—and maybe you are too—is thinking that we control more in life than we really do. When things don't go as planned, we often believe there was something we should have done to prevent it. We have trouble accepting that some of what happens to us is just part of living in a sinful world. It's not that I want you to push those thoughts away; I believe they are natural. You'll need time to work through them; but don't let them consume you. Accept that wondering "why" is normal but in the end, you'll need to come to peace with the fact that even if you discover why, it won't change your circumstances. You'll still be looking for a new job.

Know that you aren't alone. Job and his friends asked plenty of "why" questions throughout most of the book of Job. Finally, God spoke and when he did, he let Job have it. There's a lesson in this for us: *Then the Lord spoke to Job out of the storm. He said: "Who is this that obscures my plans with words without knowledge? Brace*

*yourself like a man; I will question you, and you shall answer me.
"Where were you when I laid the earth's foundation? Tell me, if you
understand. Who marked off its dimensions? Surely you know! Who
stretched a measuring line across it? On what were its footings set, or
who laid its cornerstone—while the morning stars sang together and
all the angels shouted for joy?"* (Job 38:1-7). Ouch, that's harsh,
and it was only the first of God's responses.

In the end, Job admitted that he was wrong: *Then Job replied to
the Lord: "I know that you can do all things; no purpose of yours can
be thwarted. You asked, 'Who is this that obscures my plans without
knowledge?' Surely I spoke of things I did not understand, things too
wonderful for me to know"* (Job 42:1-3).

I'm embarrassed to admit I've done it myself, asking "why"
too many times and deserving to hear what Job heard from God.
When that happens, I try looking at things from a different
perspective; I imagine my children questioning my decisions. As
a father, I see the bigger picture and know what's best for them.

The same is true for us. God our Father knows what's best. He
has amazing plans in store that he's waiting to reveal, according
to his timing, not ours. So let go of "why." Trust God and focus
on "what's next"!

WHAT WILL MY FAMILY THINK?

WHAT WILL MY FAMILY think? I need to tell them and I'm not certain what their reaction will be. It's likely you pondered this question twice—first when you initially told them the news and later as you wondered how it was affecting them. It's my prayer and hope that their reaction was one of love and understanding, because family is God's creation for a support system.

I almost cried tears of joy when I heard my family's reactions. My favorite came from my son Drew, a freshman in high school at the time. When he heard, he told my wife, "Tell Dad that San Diego is okay. So is Chicago, New York, or anywhere in Florida. But please, don't take me to Iowa." (Now, if you are from Iowa, please don't be insulted. It's a wonderful state and we even have good friends from Iowa.) The message to take from his comment was that if we needed to move, he was ready ... but his preference was for somewhere he wanted to go. If he could be positive, certainly I could too!

Personally, I don't think we give our families enough credit. It can be hard to look at this objectively when we're hurting, but I believe families understand much better than we do that bad things can and will happen. They aren't as concerned about everything you're worried about; they just love you and care for you. This is the time to let them do just that.

If you have children, then you know they look at life differently. They're probably glad to have you around more often instead of always being "at work." If your family teases you about being unemployed, learn to laugh at it. It's their way of saying "we love you." I remember a dinner table discussion about how everyone was going to get to where they needed to be the next day. Somewhere in the middle of the discussion one of my sons said, "Why is it that the person who doesn't have a job gets a car?" Everyone paused a moment for my reaction. When I laughed, they all broke up. I had set the stage that it was okay to tease a little, and they certainly did from time to time.

Take time to read 1 Corinthians 13:1-13. It's often called the chapter on love and I think verses 7, 8 and 13 are especially timely because this is what a family's love can do: *[Love] always protects, always trusts, always hopes, always perseveres. Love never fails. … And now these three remain: faith, hope and love. But the greatest of these is love.*

You can have the best job in the world; but without love, you have nothing.

TIME TO TELL THE WORLD

YOU RECENTLY LEARNED YOU no longer have a job. Now what do you do? A normal first reaction is to keep quiet, telling only your family and perhaps a few close friends. People are often embarrassed when losing a job, but when you think about it, it's odd to feel this way. After all, you didn't do anything; it just happened. I imagine it feels like getting cut from a sports team or not getting that part in the school play. You feel like a failure and most of us don't want to spread the news that we're a failure. But think about it for a moment. Good can come from telling others.

The greatest challenge you face right now is finding a new job. People need to know that you're out there looking, and I don't just mean the people where you apply for a job. I've found that people want to help, and that they like to help. But they can't help if they don't know.

A good friend told me a story about a baseball manager who had been fired. He didn't tell many people or reach out to his friends and it took him a long time to find a new job. As often happens in baseball, he got fired again. This time he threw a big party, inviting lots of friends and associates. He wanted the world to know that he was available. Guess what? He found a job much more quickly.

If you haven't already done so, create a message letting others know you are out of work and on a job search. See Appendix D for examples. Invite their prayers and their assistance. Send it to as many people as possible, whether you think they're connected and can help you find a job or not. I'm confident that two things will come from getting the word out. First, you'll receive many responses, calls or cards affirming you as a person and offering to help. Second, people will pray, and you'll need all the prayers you can get on this journey.

In Mark 16:15 we find Jesus urging his disciples to proclaim the Gospel: *[Jesus] said to them, "Go into all the world and preach the gospel to all creation."* In Matthew 28:19-20 we read, *Therefore go and make disciples of all nations, baptizing them in the name of the Father and of the Son and of the Holy Spirit, and teaching them to obey everything I have commanded you. And surely, I am with you always, to the very end of the age.* Jesus knew that people could not be saved if they didn't know the Gospel. His commandment was to "tell the world"; it wasn't to "keep silent."

While the proclamation of the Gospel exceeds my need to let others know I'm seeking a job, the principle is the same. People won't know if you don't tell them. Don't wait.

I'M ANGRY!

I'M ANGRY! I JUST want to scream! This isn't supposed to happen like this. I wasn't supposed to lose my job. It wasn't in my plans. It's not how I saw the future. I'm really pissed off. Sound familiar? Have any these thoughts come to mind lately? I think you are normal if they have, and I'd worry more if you had no anger at all.

Who are you most mad at? The person who let you go, likely your boss? The person from human resources who sat with your boss and helped deliver the message? Your coworkers? Your staff? The president of the company? The board of directors? How about the economy? Our nation's president? After all, isn't the economy his job? Congress? They pass the laws, don't they? The list is endless, but somehow we tend to come back to God. We're mad at him because he let this happen. He's God; he could have stopped it but he didn't. So let's be mad at God.

We live in an imperfect world—full of imperfect people and full of sin and pain. Because of this, bad things happen—even to good people. Our God loves you more than anyone else could ever love and care for you. Think about it. If you're a parent, what do you do when your children go through pain? You hurt for them and you probably even shed tears. I believe our Heavenly

Father has and is shedding tears at the pain you are going through because of his love for you. Could God have stopped it? Yes, he has that type of power. But remember, it is in our weakness that he is the strongest.

How do we deal with this anger? You need to get it out. First, God needs to hear your anger. He wants to hear from you and he's ready. It's probably not one conversation either; it's many. The psalmist in Psalm 55 says it's morning, noon and night that he cries out: *As for me, I call to God, and the Lord saves me. Evening, morning and noon I cry out in distress, and he hears my voice* (Psalm 55:16-17). Ask God to hear your cry of anger and to take it away. The more we cry out to God, the quicker the anger will go away and the closer we will get to him. He wants us to be close to him. We read in Psalm 145:18 that *the Lord is near to all who call on him, to all who call on him in truth.*

In your conversation with God, let him *hear all of it.* Don't pull any punches. You can't move forward until you get the anger out and that may take a few weeks; it might even take a couple of months. In Ephesians 4:26-27, we are reminded that if we stay angry, we give the devil a foothold in our heart: *In your anger do not sin: Do not let the sun go down while you are still angry, and do not give the devil a foothold.*

The devil uses your anger to doubt and not trust, to lash out and hurt others. Don't give him a chance.

HOW COULD GOD LET THIS HAPPEN?

HOW COULD GOD LET this happen? Couldn't this have happened to someone else instead of me? We ask questions like this all the time when something we don't like happens. Right now, you're probably asking them because you lost your job. I know I did when I lost mine. I still don't know the answer, except to say that this is a sinful world and bad things happen. Why did my loved one die? Why did that car stop short in front of me so that I rear-ended it? Why was that test so difficult? It's unfair! When you think about it, our lives are full of "why" questions.

While in the Garden of Gethsemane, even Jesus asked if what he was facing could be taken away, not once but three times: *Going a little farther, [Jesus] fell with his face to the ground and prayed, "My Father, if it is possible, may this cup be taken from me. Yet not as I will, but as you will." … He went away a second time and prayed, "My Father, if it is not possible for this cup to be taken away unless I drink it, may your will be done." … [He] went away once more and prayed the third time, saying the same thing* (Matthew 26:39-44). What's different here, between us and Jesus, is that he knew what was coming. We, however, can only imagine what's coming next.

Rarely do we ask God "why" when something good happens. When was the last time you said, "Hey God, why did you send that blessing my way?" It's as if we think we should get only the good things and never the bad. Job had a great response to this in Job 2:10 when he replied, *You are talking like a foolish woman. Shall we accept good from God, and not trouble?* The verse goes on to say that *in all this, Job did not sin in what he said.* We need to take heed and accept the troubles of this world right along with the good.

In Romans 8:28, we are reminded that God can take what we consider a disaster and work something good from it: *And we know that **in all things** God works for the good of those who love him, who have been called according to his purpose.* The Apostle Paul who wrote these words had disastrous things happen to him, but he clung to God's promises that he's with us; we are his children; he'll take care of us; he'll make something good from what has happened.

It is in looking back that we often see the wonder and majesty of God and how he has taken care of us. During my journey, I spoke to many who had been previously unemployed. I heard the same thing over and over: "It wasn't fun by any stretch, but it turned out to be the best thing for me." I must agree; it was for me, too. I experienced things I would never have dreamed or imagined had my eyes not been opened to all God could provide.

If God had intervened and I'd have kept my job, the blessings of the future would never have happened. He knows what's best and he will not forsake you in this difficult time. The reason this happened doesn't matter; just trust that God knows what's best for you.

A TIME FOR EVERYTHING?
WHAT TIME IS IT NOW?

ECCLESIASTES 3:1-8 IS WORTH reading or rereading, especially at this time in your life: *There is a time for everything, and a season for every activity under heaven: a time to be born and a time to die, a time to plant and a time to uproot, a time to kill and a time to heal, a time to tear down and a time to build, a time to weep and a time to laugh, a time to mourn and a time to dance, a time to scatter stones and a time to gather them, a time to embrace and a time to refrain from embracing, a time to search and a time to give up, a time to keep and a time to throw away, a time to tear and a time to mend, a time to be silent and a time to speak, a time to love and a time to hate, a time for war and a time for peace.*

Even as these verses remind us that there is a time for everything, you may be thinking I'm a little lost right now. What do I do with this time? It can be difficult to enjoy this time because of the pressure to find a new job. Work is often so much a part of our lives that we don't know what to do without it. There is no "rulebook" for being unemployed. I looked and looked and looked for something that would tell me how I should act, what I should think, and how I should spend my time. I never did find it. We sometimes think such rules exist, but they are nothing more than what we believe "others" think we should do. And if we spend our time worrying about what others think, we won't help ourselves at all. Remember, this journey is personal to you, no one else.

Yes, there is a time to work but it's okay to experience a time to be unemployed. What do you do with this time of unemployment? I've discovered there are many things we don't take enough time to do, things that are more important than what we do as a job. Make a list and check them off as you go. Here are some to consider:

- Think about the gifts God has given you.
- Reflect on what gives you the most joy.
- Slow down and enjoy the simple things of life.
- Visit friends.
- Be with your family, your spouse, your children, your grandchildren (a special type of fun).
- Let the stress of what you're going through ease.
- Enjoy a hobby.
- Read Scripture.
- Be still and listen for God's direction.
- Pray.

Embrace this change, this gift of time. You may never have this type of time again until you retire, so make the most of it and enjoy its unexpected blessings.

WHAT ABOUT FINANCES?

"HOW WILL WE EVER make it financially without me working?" This question probably comes to mind for everyone, regardless of how much money you make, what you have saved in a bank account, or how long you might have some severance pay coming to you. It certainly came to me.

The devil loves it when we feel insecure, when faith and trust in God wavers. Money makes us feel secure, lack of it insecure. Losing your job could pose a big financial challenge or even a crisis and the devil wants you to believe that this "crisis" can't be managed. But stop for a moment. Take out a dollar bill and look at it. Find the phrase "In God We Trust." It doesn't say "trust in this currency"; it says trust "in God." How ironic.

Where will you put your trust? Let's look in Deuteronomy 8:18 for where our wealth comes from in the first place: *But remember the Lord your God, for it is he who gives you the ability to produce wealth, and so confirms his covenant, which he swore to your ancestors, as it is today.* Our wealth isn't ours; it comes from God. We are simply stewards of what he has given to us. As good stewards, we should evaluate and possibly cut back on spending.

As tempting as it may be when it comes to what you give

to God, I urge you to *not cut back on giving to the Lord*. Don't think of it as an "expense category" that needs to be reevaluated. Whatever income you are receiving from severance pay or unemployment, make your offering the first check you write. Years ago, my pastor and good friend Vern asked a question of me when I admitted we weren't tithing. He said, "Dale, what will make you trust God more that will allow you to give a tithe (10%)?" That was a tough question; I had no answer.

Here's what God says in Malachi 3:10: *"Bring the whole tithe into the storehouse, that there may be food in my house.* **Test me in this**," *says the Lord Almighty, "and see if I will not throw open the floodgates of heaven and pour out so much blessing that there will not be room enough to store it."* I can tell you that we indeed tested him and then experienced God pouring out his blessings. We discovered that with God's blessings, 90% of whatever income we have goes farther than 100% without them.

God invites you to trust him to be your provider. I doubt you'll ever find a former "tither," one who used to tithe but no longer does. I never have, and I don't think I ever will, because of how graciously he blesses us when we respond to his love by giving back what he's already given to us.

Step out in faith without relying on your own math. Rely on God's math; trust him, and you'll be amazed at the riches of his blessings.

I THINK I SCREWED UP;
NOW WHAT?

YOU MIGHT BELIEVE THAT you screwed up and that you're responsible, partially or totally, for losing your job. Maybe; maybe not. It's possible you did contribute, but it's also possible that what you think you did had no impact at all, and that it wasn't even a factor. Rarely, if ever, are we told all the reasons that led to the decision regarding your job. Let's assume for this moment, however, that something you did was indeed a factor. What now?

We all make mistakes and can recover. This personal race of life you are running isn't a sprint, where one fall impacts your success. It's a marathon and there's plenty of time for God to help you recover. Statistically speaking, chances are pretty good that no one died or was physically harmed from what you did. The real question to ask is where do you go from here? The answer lies within you.

The first step is confession. Keep in mind that we aren't perfect and it's a big mistake to think we can be. In 1 John 1:8-9 we read, *if we claim to be without sin, we deceive ourselves and the truth is not in us. If we confess our sins, [God] is faithful and just and will forgive us our sins and purify us from all unrighteousness.* Be honest with God about what happened and ask for his forgiveness, help and guidance. He is a forgiving God; his mercy and grace are amazing.

The hard part comes next—forgetting about the mistake and no longer beating yourself up. We often say (or at least I do), "Thanks for forgiving me, but I think I'll still beat myself up because I wasn't perfect." Well, when God forgives, he also forgets. In Psalm 103:12 the psalmist describes God's forgiveness like this: *As far as the east is from the west, so far has he removed our transgressions from us.* If God can forgive and forget, shouldn't we be able to do it with ourselves?

Take some time to consider what you learned from what happened. Did you respond in haste, not choose your words carefully, didn't double check your work, or …? The learning is the most important part. We all make mistakes; what's important is that we not keep making the same ones. If a potential employer should ask what you've learned, be prepared to answer honestly. If you failed to do something, admit it and immediately follow up with how you'll do better. Employers want honesty and know that employees make mistakes. It's how people react to their mistakes that's important.

Remember that you aren't alone, the world is full of people who make mistakes. Accept God's forgiveness and his grace. Then move on.

THE FUTURE: PART 1

I WALKED INTO THE kitchen of our best friends' home. It was shortly after learning my job was being eliminated. A sign was taped on Don and Cheryl's kitchen counter with these words:

I DON'T KNOW WHAT THE FUTURE HOLDS,
BUT I KNOW WHO HOLDS THE FUTURE!

They told me they'd had it there for some time; it wasn't for me. Yet I felt that God was speaking to me and I loved it. What an appropriate message for starting this journey. I don't know what the future holds for me or for you. The unknown can be scary, and it can be exciting. As I look to my future, here's what I do know.

God didn't promise you or me a life without challenge; we will have them and each challenge is a test. This period of unemployment will test me, and it will test you. But we'll be better and stronger having gone through it: *Consider it pure joy, my brothers and sisters, whenever you face trials of many kinds, because you know that the testing of your faith produces perseverance. Let perseverance finish its work so that you may be mature and complete, not lacking anything. If any of you lacks wisdom, you should ask*

God, who gives generously to all without finding fault, and it will be given to you. But when you ask, you must believe and not doubt, because the one who doubts is like a wave of the sea, blown and tossed by the wind (James 1:2-6).

I know that God is right beside me on this journey and he's right beside you. It's good to know that in the most challenging times we have a helper alongside us, one who will never leave us as we are reminded in Hebrews 13:5-6. *Keep your lives free from the love of money and be content with what you have, because God has said, "Never will I leave you; never will I forsake you." So we say with confidence, "The Lord is my helper; I will not be afraid. What can mere mortals do to me?"*

I have learned from experience that when something we don't expect happens and we're especially challenged, that God uses *all* things—the good and bad—to shape us and prepare us. Good things will come out of this change, because that's exactly what he tells us in Romans 8:28. *And we know that in **all** things God works for the good of those who love him, who have been called according to his purpose.*

Move forward in this journey knowing that God is with you; he won't leave you and all things will work to the good for you.

ALLOWING FOR GOD'S AMAZING GRACE

GOD'S GRACE IS TRULY amazing—he gives us what we do not deserve, his unending love. And he calls us to extend that love—his grace—to others. I have a good friend, Sally, who always tells me to look for "God's amazing grace." I've seen many examples of God's grace on my journeys through unemployment. I believe you will too, if you look.

One of my challenges, and maybe yours too, is accepting the kindness of others and letting them love me. I believe that too often personal pride gets in the way. We might view a person who is "being loved" (receiving the grace) as less equal. After all, it's more fun to be the giver of grace than to be the receiver, or so we think. However, Scripture warns that God doesn't approve of pride. Instead, he wants us to be humble and open to being loved: *But [God] gives us more grace. That is why Scripture says: "God opposes the proud but shows favor to the humble"* (James 4:6).

*It is good for our hearts to be strengthened by grace (*Hebrews 13:9). God's grace strengthens us for each of the challenges we face. Think back to when you were young. When you were emotionally or physically hurt, what did you do? You ran to

Mom or Dad so they could love on you. They made it all feel better. You can also go to God with your current hurts and struggles and let him love on you. He'll do it through others. I believe you'll have many people on your journey ready to show you a special kindness—God's amazing grace—and I hope you'll accept it.

How might this happen? A friend meets with you for breakfast or lunch to talk about your journey. The check comes and instinctively you want to pick up the check and pay for it, but your friend grabs it first. You could pay—you have money or maybe, in your previous role, you always picked up the check. Stop. Accept letting someone do that for you. Others want to do it for any number of reasons. They realize you are struggling and want to do something kind for you. Or maybe they've been in your shoes and this is their way of paying back someone who did it for them. Most of all, they care.

Who knows what other unexpected kindnesses—reminders of God's amazing grace—you'll receive along this journey? It might be the free use of someone's condo in a resort area for a "getaway," a gift card to a favorite restaurant, or an invitation to a special sporting event. There are endless ways for God's amazing grace to come to you. He wants you to enjoy it. It's his way of saying "I love you" through others. You didn't earn these special acts of kindness, because if you had earned them, they wouldn't be grace.

God's amazing grace is awesome; enjoy being loved.

FAITH IS A MUSCLE

I'M CONVINCED THAT FAITH is a muscle. What I know about muscles is that if you don't use them, they waste away. It's called *atrophy*. You can look up what the dictionary says about atrophy, but to me it can be summed up in the old expression "If you don't use it, you'll lose it."

I also believe the same can be true for faith. We often try to play it safe and avoid risk in our lives. We try to make our imperfect world "perfect," free from challenge and hardship. I get that. Who wants pain? Most of us don't. But I also know that through pain and hardship, our faith experiences the most tremendous growth.

At some point, we all experience crisis. You're in one of those now. When in crisis, we often look to God to bail us out, to fix the problem. God does help us, but he does it in his own way, not ours. Which also means according to his timing (I hate that one), not ours. He wants to teach us to put our trust in him and to have faith that he'll deliver.

I listened to a John O'Leary podcast, a nationally recognized speaker who suffered a terrible accident as a young boy. He was interviewing Joel Boggess, an author and motivational speaker who at the age of five suffered a devastating accident. As Joel told his story, he said something that stuck with me. He said, "Faith doesn't grow without action on my part." When I heard those words, I knew he was right.

James 2:17 spells out the importance of action. *In the same way, **faith by itself, if it is not accompanied by action, is dead**.* You can't sit on your couch at home saying, "I have faith God will find a new job for me." That's not faith, that's stupid. You and I will have to do things we don't like to do, things we aren't comfortable doing, as part of the job search. In doing those things, we step out in faith, exercising our trust in God. Hebrews chapter 11 is often referred to as the "faith chapter." I encourage you to read all of it and focus on the actions of those mentioned. Here are a couple examples: *By faith Abel brought God a better offering* (verse 4); *By faith Abraham, when called to go to a place he would later receive as his inheritance, obeyed and went, even though he did not know where he was going* (verse 8).

Actions exercise our faith muscles. The more we use them, the stronger they get. How do you know they are getting stronger? We experience the peace and contentment that comes from trusting in God. Also, please don't worry about trying to be perfect in your actions; once you get started, one of two things will happen. God will either bless the direction of our actions, or he'll redirect them.

So get up and start exercising those faith muscles.

DON'T SPEAK POORLY OF OTHERS

IT'S A GOOD POSSIBILITY that when you were told you no longer have a job—regardless of the reason—the person delivering the news said, "It's not personal." And for those who make or execute such decisions, it really isn't "personal." When he or she told you that, they were referring to their intent. I'm certain no one woke up that day and said, "Let's hurt [insert your name] by taking away their job." Your organization made its decision and believed it was the right decision. To them, it wasn't personal.

But for me and for you, it is "personal" because of the impact it has on us and those we love. We're hurt. We don't have a job and we don't know what's next. When we're hurt, we often want to lash out at those who hurt us. The challenge is that it's hard to hurt an organization, so the most common avenue we choose is to use words. You might say to yourself, "I'll spread the word about those terrible people who did this to me. I'll write a letter to the board of directors. I'll …"

Please stop right there and *don't do it!* It's not good to do it. It's not right to do it. It won't help anything. It won't change what happened. Have you ever read Ephesians 4:29? *Do not let any unwholesome talk come out of your mouths, but only what is helpful for building others up according to their needs, that it may benefit those who listen.*

Let those words sink in. Only say things that build up others, not tear them down, no matter what the circumstances. Yes, even when they've hurt you. What do you really hope to gain by speaking ill about them? You might think you'll feel better, but really you won't. In the end, it says more about you as a person than it does about any of the individuals you're talking about or the organization itself. In Romans 2:1 we read, *You, therefore, have no excuse, you who pass judgment on someone else, for at whatever point you judge another, you are condemning yourself, because you who pass judgment do the same things.* This text tells us that when we do something such as speaking poorly of others, we end up making ourselves look bad.

It's time to let it go and only speak good of the organization and the people who made the decision. If they did it poorly, others will know without you telling them. One last thing to keep in mind about speaking negatively: What would you want them to say about you?

Practice the golden rule as laid out for us in Matthew 7:12: *So in everything, do to others what you would have them do to you, for this sums up the Law and the Prophets.* If you want others to speak well of you, speak well of them.

WHERE IS MY PROTECTOR?

HAVE YOU EVER HAD a protector, other than your parents? Someone who watched over you? Maybe your older brother or sister did that for you. In work, we sometimes have a mentor, someone we turn to who helps and shapes us. Someone who also is a protector, keeping us from making big mistakes. I've had both—an older brother and a few mentors. And I can tell you it's nice to have a protector.

Right now, you're on a journey into the unknown. Your life is changing. You don't know where God is leading you next. You don't know when you'll get your next job, what you'll be doing or where you'll be doing it. Everything is unknown. If you're like most people, the unknown scares us. I know it scares me. Think of this as an opportunity to learn to embrace the unknown. Yikes, you say? I don't like the unknown and you want me to embrace it?!?!

I recently saw this post from Kim and very much liked what it had to say:

THE WILL OF GOD WILL NOT TAKE YOU
WHERE THE GRACE OF GOD WILL NOT PROTECT YOU!

That's good to know. Wherever I go—even into the unknown, into something new—I have God as my protector. This statement summarizes one of my favorite passages in Scripture, Isaiah 43:1-3, 5-7. *But now, this is what the Lord says—he who created you, Jacob, he who formed you, Israel: "Do not fear, for I have redeemed you; I have summoned you by name; you are mine. When you pass through the waters, I will be with you; and when you pass through the rivers, they will not sweep over you. When you walk through the fire, you will not be burned; the flames will not set you ablaze. For I am the Lord your God, the Holy One of Israel, your Savior ... Do not be afraid, for I am with you; I will bring your children from the east and gather you from the west. I will say to the north, 'Give them up!' and to the south, 'Do not hold them back.' Bring my sons from afar and my daughters from the ends of the earth— everyone who is called by my name, whom I created for my glory, whom I formed and made."*

Here we are reminded that we are God's children. He promises to be with us in all our trials (through this big change in your life) and troubles, so they need not overwhelm us. He goes on to remind us that he is the Lord our God and he'll do anything for us.

He is our protector on the journey: we can relax.

I DON'T DESERVE THIS

I DON'T DESERVE THIS! I imagine you said something like this shortly after learning you'd be out of work. If you didn't say it, certainly a good friend or coworker probably said it to you. Maybe neither you nor I deserved to lose our job. Unfortunately, though, we live in a world where bad things happen to good people. You and I weren't the first and we won't be the last. I hear stories all the time of people who lost their jobs and probably didn't deserve it.

If you pick up your Bible and do a little reading, you'll find that your situation isn't even as bad as what some others went through, much of which they didn't deserve. Here are just a few:

Jesus was crucified for no reason, no crime. *[Pilate] said to them, "You brought me this man as one who was inciting the people to rebellion. I have examined him in your presence and have found no basis for your charges against him* (Luke 23:14). John the Baptist was beheaded (Matthew 14:1-12), Job lost his family (Job 1, 2:1-10). Joseph was sold by his brothers into slavery (Genesis 37-45). Jacob worked seven years to marry Rachel, then was tricked into marrying her sister and had to work another seven to marry Rachel (Genesis 29:1-30). Esau's brother Jacob stole his blessing from their father (Genesis 27:1-40).

In Job 1:21 we are reminded that nothing is ours on our own; it's all God's. *[Job] said: "Naked I came from my mother's womb, and naked I will depart. The Lord gave and the Lord has taken away; may the name of the Lord be praised."*

The job I had wasn't "mine"; it was a gift from God. Yours was also a gift. It's unfortunate those gifts were taken away, but here's something important to keep in mind: Whether something is deserved or not ***does not change that it happened***. You are still unemployed. The question is how you will deal with it from this point on.

You have some choices to make. You can let this get you down; you can quit. Or you can move past what happened, make the best of it, and move forward to see what great things God has in store for you.

I encourage you to move forward, taking to heart these words from the Apostle Paul written while in prison: *Brothers and sisters, I do not consider myself yet to have taken hold of it. But one thing I do: Forgetting what is behind and straining toward what is ahead, I press on toward the goal to win the prize for which God has called me heavenward in Christ Jesus* (Philippians 3:13-14).

COMMUNICATION AND EXPECTATIONS ARE REQUIRED

THE RELATIONSHIP YOU HAVE with a significant other, such as a spouse or a person you're in a serious relationship with, has just changed. If you aren't in such a relationship, the one you have with family and close friends has changed. Your entire world has changed because you're in a job search and not working. But life seems normal for your spouse, partner, family, or friends. My experience, however, has taught me that it is now different *for everyone* involved, even if they don't know it or express it.

Everyone has some expectation of what they "think" your journey will look like, how long your job search should take, what you should be doing, etc. We rarely talk about those expectations, but if they're unrealistic, or what's going on is different than what's expected, conflict can happen. I once met someone on a job search who got up each day, dressed as if he were going to work and went to a local café for breakfast and to read the paper. Why? Because his spouse didn't think he was doing anything to find a job if he didn't get up as normal and get out of the house. Clearly, these two had not talked enough about the search, what was being done and how the process would happen.

Start early with a good conversation about expectations. You need to be honest and not tell each other what you "think" they need or want to hear. Share openly about what each of you thinks should happen. If you don't know, then say you don't know. Share your fears and anxieties. Come to a common understanding for getting started and accept that there may be changes as you move through the process.

Then, if you don't already have a routine for doing so, make sure you take a weekly time out (away from the children if you have them at home) to enjoy each other and to relieve the stress of this journey. When you're out, take time to talk and to listen, processing together the "ups" and "downs" of the week.

One final caution for you and those with whom you are in a relationship: Don't focus too much on what other people tell you "should" happen; it's not their life. Consider Mark 10:9: *Therefore, what God has joined together, let no one separate.* This is a vulnerable time and outside influences and comments from others can damage a relationship. The devil loves that and he knows that if your relationship is weak with those you love, it'll be hard to have the relationship you need with God.

A strong, Christ-centered relationship will give you strength and perseverance. It's what you need so that God can grow you together rather than apart. This is what God wants for you.

THE FUTURE: PART 2

IN ADDITION TO THE thoughts shared in Part 1, here are three important things to remember on this journey:

- Life isn't perfect; we will have troubles and those are tests for us.
- God never leaves us during those troubles; he's with us every step.
- No matter how difficult the challenge we face, God will use it for good.

As we journey into the future, we need to look forward, not backward. Just because you lost your job, it doesn't mean that you forget the people and the good things you experienced. It does mean you have to keep moving forward and you can't do that well if you're looking backward. These words from Philippians 3:13-14 remind us of that: *Brothers and sisters, I do not consider myself yet to have taken hold of it. But one thing I do:* ***Forgetting what is behind and straining toward what is ahead***, *I press on toward the goal to win the prize for which God has called me heavenward in Christ Jesus.* Don't quit; don't give up. Keep moving forward.

God is amazing, he has provided me with blessings beyond what I could have ever imagined and continues to do so. If you stopped to make a list of all the blessings and all the challenges in your life, the blessings would be far more than the challenges. I often make the mistake of putting limits on what God can do for me. I often don't dream enough. Think on these words from Ephesians 3:20. *Now to him who is able to do **immeasurably more than all we ask or imagine**, according to his power that is at work within us, to him be the glory.* Think about that. God is saying, "Dream your biggest dream and I can top that."

Finally, whatever we face, I know that God has prepared us for it even though we don't know what it is. One of my favorite Scriptures is Hebrews 13:20-21, where we are reminded that God will equip us with all that we need. *Now may the God of peace, who through the blood of the eternal covenant brought back from the dead our Lord Jesus, that great Shepherd of the sheep, equip you with everything good for doing his will, and may he work in us what is pleasing to him, through Jesus Christ, to whom be glory for ever and ever. Amen.*

As you look to the future, be excited. Dream big; God has your future in the palm of his hands.

POURING OUT OUR HEARTS TO GOD

I'M AT A TIME and place in my life that I don't want to be in, I'm unemployed. I didn't ask for it and I don't particularly like it. It has upset my world as I know it. I'm frustrated and I'm impatient. What do I do? How long will it last?

In times like this, God wants us to pour out our hearts to him. Tell him everything that's on our mind, what's on our heart. Look through the book of Psalms. In many of the psalms, the writer is crying out to God in pain or anguish. A frequent author of psalms was King David. If it was okay for the greatest king in all of Israel's history to cry out to God, I think I can too. Let's look at some verses from different psalms.

Let's start with Psalm 50:15. ... *and call on me in the day of trouble; I will deliver you, and you will honor me.* We aren't told to call upon God and *maybe* he'll deliver us, we're told he ***will*** deliver us. What good news for me to hear; he'll rescue me from the challenge I'm facing. It also reminds me that when it happens, to honor him for what he's done. In other words, tell the world what God has done for me; and when it happens for you, tell them it was God who did this for you.

When should we cry out? Look at Psalm 55:16-17. *As for me, I call to God, and the Lord saves me. Evening, morning and noon I cry out in distress, and he hears my voice.* Here we're told that it's okay to keep crying out, all the time. The psalmist cried out "evening, morning and noon," which I take to be all the time. God wants to know what distresses us, our fears and our concerns. What makes each of us anxious? Is it money you're worried about? What others think of you? Your cries will be different from mine; but whatever they are, he wants to hear them.

God doesn't want us to "sugarcoat" what we have to say either. So, at times, I cry out like in Psalm 4:1. *Answer me when I call to you, my righteous God. Give me relief from my distress; have mercy on me and hear my prayer.* For me this might look like this: God, please give me relief from this stress. Please give me a new job, one that I'll love, one that uses my gifts.

Another cry of mine was that of David's, and maybe yours too, from Psalm 6:3. *My soul is in anguish. How long, O Lord, how long?* That cry comes when I don't do well with waiting. I keep asking, when, God, will this end?

Whatever is on your heart and mind, pour it out to God. He's there and ready to listen.

GOD ALLOWED THIS TO HAPPEN

I'M HAVING A "CUP of coffee" with Michael at a local coffee shop. As I sit with him, it's the 19th "cup of coffee" (which doesn't include breakfasts or lunches) I've had with someone on my journey. We're at a Kaldi's today, which is in second place, not surprisingly behind Starbuck's. And I don't drink coffee. It's hot chocolate or a Diet Coke for me. It doesn't matter where we were, it's what Michael said that was important.

I served for several years on Michael's board in his previous job. He worked for city government and recently a new mayor was elected. The new mayor wanted their own team in certain positions and very quickly Michael was out of a job. As we were talking about his departure, he made a very simple comment that struck me when he said, "God allowed this to happen." He went on to say that "God could have stopped it, but he didn't." He went on to say that he was okay with the change because he understood how jobs connected to political leaders worked. More importantly, he knew God had a plan for him. He was fortunate that it didn't take long for him to land somewhere else and he had a wonderful new job and is flourishing in it.

In 1 Kings 11, God was angry with Solomon, but he told him he would hold off the punishment during his lifetime. *So the Lord said to Solomon, "Since this is your attitude and you have not kept my covenant and my decrees, which I commanded you, I will most certainly tear the kingdom away from you and give it to one of your subordinates. Nevertheless, for the sake of David your father, I will not do it during your lifetime."*

Early in the book of Job, God allowed the devil to do things to Job, but he set limits on what he would allow. *The Lord said to Satan, "Very well, then, everything he has is in your power, but on the man himself do not lay a finger"* (Job 1:12). *The Lord said to Satan, "Very well, then, he is in your hands; but you must spare his life"* (Job 2:6).

Nothing in this world happens that God doesn't know about and has approved for it to happen. When bad things happen to us, like the loss of a job, it doesn't mean God did this on purpose. It means that sin and the "free will" of humans to do things that sometimes aren't part of his plan for us exist in this world. But whatever happens—in my case losing my job—he allowed it to happen. Why did he let it happen? I don't know. Was it intentional on his part or unintentional? I don't know. I can waste hours upon hours, and days upon days, trying to figure it out and I'll never really know why.

What I do know is that he will use this experience to shape me for his purpose and draw me closer to him. Good will come out of this. He'll do the same for you.

DON'T CONSTRAIN GOD

IT WAS EASTER SUNDAY during my "sabbatical" time, still looking and waiting for God's direction on what's next. Our pastor, Scott, was preaching and his words struck home. He said that we as humans, like the disciples, often "constrain God." We put limits on God and what he can do for us. We view the world through "our reality" of what we see and know from our experiences. His example was the disciples, whom Jesus had told that he would be killed and rise again, but they didn't believe. They had seen him raise Lazarus from the dead, but their view of reality was that it had all ended on the cross on Good Friday. Their view and our view often doesn't match "God's reality," which is beyond anything we can imagine.

When I heard those words, I realized I too sometimes constrain God, especially on this job search. Maybe you've done it too. I don't do it intentionally, but I know I've done it. How do I constrain God? I believe I don't dream big enough dreams and then I compound it by not believing he can fulfill the dreams I have. I think it's a natural reaction to what's happened in the past. We tend to remember the painful and difficult times in life more than we remember the good times. I was emotionally hurt when I lost my job. There's a good chance you were hurt too. Once hurt, we don't want that to happen again, so we try to protect our emotions. If I dream small dreams, there is a better chance God can fulfill that dream and I won't be disappointed. Notice how I put a limit on God, constraining him and his power. Yikes!

But our God is a God of limitless power. He can do anything he wants to do. He wants my dreams and he wants them to be big dreams. Don't dream to find "a job"; dream the dream that is "the job you've always wanted." Scripture is full of God's promises to us, let me share three with you.

In 1 John 5:14-15, he says "ask anything" of him, not ask what seems reasonable. *This is the confidence we have in approaching God: that if we ask anything according to his will, he hears us. And if we know that he hears us—whatever we ask—we know that we have what we asked of him.*

God has something amazing in store for me and you. In 1 Corinthians 2:9 we're told it's beyond what can be imagined. *However, as it is written: "What no eye has seen, what no ear has heard, and what no human mind has conceived" the things God has prepared for those who love him.* Love God and believe in him.

During your struggles on this journey, remember that nothing is impossible for God. *For nothing is impossible with God* (Luke 1:37). So, take your constraints off God, dream big dreams, pray for them and then believe he can do it for you!

WHO AM I, NOW THAT I'M UNEMPLOYED?

"HI, I'M DALE KREIENKAMP, head of human resources for …" Very often, that's how I would introduce myself. My introduction, and maybe yours, identified me with where I worked and what I did for a living. But how about now, when I don't have a job? Who am I today?

It's a great question and one I searched for answers to. At first, I wasn't as quick to introduce myself as I'd been in the past, maybe shying away a little. I'm not normally shy; I'm an extrovert. I just felt awkward about what to say because I could no longer say what I had said for years. When I tell people I'm in between jobs, the reactions vary. For many, it's like telling them you have cancer. They don't know what to say and they certainly don't want it to happen to them. For some, it kills the conversation. Most, however, are sympathetic and want to help—they just don't know how.

Often it was me putting others at ease, assuring them everything would be okay. It gave me a chance to share my faith, telling them I believed in God and that I trusted he had a great plan for me. During this journey, I began to realize that too much of me had been wrapped up in *what I did and who I worked for*, neither of which are the most important things in life.

In Sheila Walsh's book, *Life is Tough, But God Is Faithful*, she talks about the time a growth on her vocal cord required that she cancel a concert tour. She faced the possibility of an operation and never singing again. It was a tough blow and she spent many hours in prayer, but what she revealed about the experience was what I needed most to hear. She writes, "I got the distinct impression that God was saying, Sheila, don't you understand that I love you because of who you are and not for what you do? Your security has been all wrapped up in thinking of yourself as Sheila Walsh the singer, the evangelist, the speaker, the person who goes out there and does it all for Me. But that's not why I love you. If you never sing another note, it will not matter to Me. I don't need you to do things for Me. I just really love you." That is so perfectly said.

One of my favorite passages in the Bible is Ephesians 2:8-10, which reads, *It is by grace you have been saved, through faith—and this is not from yourselves, it is the gift of God—not by works, so that no one can boast. For we are God's handiwork, created in Christ Jesus to do good works, which God prepared in advance for us to do.* Our identity is not found in what we do, but in what God has done for us. It's about God's grace, not what we do—and that can be hard to accept. We are God's handiwork; in return whatever we do is done in thankful response to his love.

Take this time to let God love you for who you are, not for what you did in your old job or what you will do in your next. It's not who you are; it's whose you are.

WHAT ARE YOUR GIFTS?

YOU HAVE AN OPPORTUNITY to do something we don't usually take time to do; please don't miss it. I'm serious; this is a chance to ask yourself some key questions about work. When you become unemployed, the first thing you think about or someone tells you to do is to update your resume. While this is indeed important, I believe the most important thing is to consider your gifts—what you do well, what brings you *joy* in your work. Too many people are working but not experiencing joy because their job doesn't match their gifts.

Let's look at 1 Peter 4:10. *Each of you should use whatever gift you have received to serve others, as faithful stewards of God's grace in its various forms.* We can draw three things from this text which are important for your job search.

"Use whatever gifts you have received." God doesn't say hide your gifts; he says to use them. That can mean finding a job that offers the opportunity to use your gifts every day, not once a month or once a year. I imagine you, like me, can learn how to do many things. But the difference between the ability to do something and a gift is the level of joy and excitement it brings. I'm analytical and good with numbers, but they don't bring joy or excitement. That's not how I want to use my time.

Too often we ignore this part of a job search because we feel panicked about getting back to work to earn money. But I urge you to take the time to ask your friends, family, and former coworkers what they see as your gifts. Write them on a piece of paper. As you consider applying for different jobs, ask yourself if the job offers the opportunity to use the gifts you identified. If you won't be using your gifts, why consider the job?

Next, the text says we ought to use these gifts to *serve others*. If it's really a gift, you'll be helping others in using it. In the work environment, using your gifts will make the team you work on better than without you. Those you serve—your customers—will benefit because your gifts are being used.

The third thing is to be *faithful stewards*. To be a faithful steward of your gift, you must take care of it. You can't do that by ignoring a gift or hiding it. One of the ways we exhibit stewardship is to use the gifts God has given us.

I believe God wants us to have joy in what we do for a living. On your journey, look for jobs that let you use your gifts, regardless of the money you'll make. After all, money won't provide long-term satisfaction; it's something we never think we have enough of. But when you're doing something that uses your gifts, the joy you receive and share with others will reap wonderful rewards.

DARK DAYS

IT'S A "DARK DAY" today as I write this. What's a "dark day"? It's a day when the feelings you don't want to feel seem to dominate. It's a day when you experience discouragement, dejection, hopelessness, loneliness, helplessness or any other negative emotion you can think of. It's hard to predict when they'll come or how long they'll stay. And, I'm sorry to say, they'll come no matter what you do to prevent them. They will come because the devil likes us to have them, which is why there's nothing we can to do prevent them. Today is one of those days.

The "dark days" for me come when I lose focus. Not my focus on getting things done related to my job search, but my focus on Jesus. Have you read Matthew 14:22-33 lately? It's the story of the disciples out in their boat in the middle of the night when Jesus comes to them on the water. Peter says, "If it's you, Lord, I'll come to you." Jesus tells Peter to come, so he got out of the boat and started walking on the water toward Jesus. Wow, everything was good! He was doing what seemed impossible and I imagine he felt great at that moment.

Then he did what we often do, certainly what I've done. He took his focus off Jesus and looked at what was around him. It frightened him, and he started to sink. *"Lord, if it's you,"* Peter *replied, "tell me to come to you on the water." "Come," he said. Then Peter got down out of the boat, walked on the water and came toward Jesus. But when he saw the wind, he was afraid and, beginning to sink, cried out, "Lord, save me!" Immediately Jesus reached out his hand and caught him. "You of little faith," he said, "why did you doubt?"* (Matthew 14:28-31).

Jesus wants you to focus on him through this process, not on the world around you. As much as others want to help you and care for you, they are bound to say things that will make you lose focus. They will want you to be "realistic," so they might say things like "it took me nine months to find a job" or "at your age it's going to be tough to find a job" or "you might need to change industries" or "if you don't do ___ it'll be very hard to find a job," etc. And if you stop and think about those things, you just might say "they might be right." Once you start believing that, you lose focus and it gets very, very scary.

Today I took my eyes off Jesus, looking too far into the future and asking myself "what if?" I got scared, and then he said to me what he said to Peter: "You of little faith, why did you doubt?" My answer was that I was trying to be you, solving my own problem. I'm human and I'm sorry.

When your dark days come, refocus on Jesus, not what you hear or see in this world. Remember, he is our God who can do anything, fix any problem, any concern, any obstacle.

Focus on him and the darkness will disappear.

I CAN'T LET GO OF THE HURT

FOR SOME OF YOU, your hurt will be so extreme, it will be difficult to let it go. You're so angry with those who hurt you that you spend many hours thinking about them and reviewing what happened, time and time again. You think about it when you're driving, watching TV, and even while lying in bed, not sleeping. I'll certainly admit I've had days when these things dominated my thoughts. It's a normal part of the process. The challenge we face is that we can't move on until we let go of the past and our hurt.

Over the years I've met with many individuals who were in between jobs and were networking with me. For a few, the hurt and anger were so evident in how they looked and acted that I had to tell them I couldn't recommend anything *until* they can let go of the past. How you handle what happened tells more about *you* than it does about your previous employer. A prospective employer won't hire someone with a negative attitude about their past employer because they don't want it to enter their workplace.

So what do you do about it? I was having a cup of coffee with Ron, who recently found a new job. We were talking about the process and the different people we meet along the way. Ron said he was lucky that he was able to let go of what happened to him relatively quickly, but that he often finds people who say they've let go, but they keep working negative comments into the conversation about how they were treated. He told me that when this happens, he suggests that the person pray for those who hurt them.

Ron pointed out that it's hard to hold a grudge against someone you are praying for, and he's right. That's excellent advice and I've practiced it myself. How about you? Have you prayed for those who hurt you? Have you forgiven them? In Mark 11:24-25 we read these words of Jesus: *Therefore I tell you, whatever you ask for in prayer, believe that you have received it, and it will be yours. And when you stand praying, if you hold anything against anyone, forgive them, so that your Father in heaven may forgive you your sins.* If we hold a grudge and don't forgive, how can we ask God to forgive our sins?

Forgiving doesn't mean forgetting. I'm not saying you need to invite those who hurt you to your house for dinner or a party. You might not be able to forget what happened but over time, forgiving means that it can stop bringing hurt. Consider these words of the psalmist: *May these words of my mouth and this meditation of my heart be pleasing in your sight, Lord, my Rock and my Redeemer* (Psalm 19:14).

Think about what's on your heart and mind. Let go and forgive as God forgives.

HE COMES TO US

I WAS INTRODUCED TO Benjamin by a good friend Bill and was blessed to have coffee with him. As most of my networking conversations go, it started with learning more about what Benjamin was doing and about him, the person. We talked about my search and what I was looking for. Toward the end of our time together I became extra excited with our conversation as Benjamin opened the door for me to talk about this book and then made a comment that in times like this (my period of unemployment) God comes to us. I was particularly interested in this comment since our normal reaction is to ask, "Where is God now?" "How could he let this happen?" or "Why did he let this happen?" Benjamin is a man of faith and the son of a minister. He then gave me a lesson helpful to all of us.

Look at Matthew 14 and the story of Jesus walking on the water, starting with verse 23. *Later that night, he was there alone, and the boat was already a considerable distance from land, buffeted by the waves because the wind was against it.* The disciples were in a small boat, in open water, in a storm. That's not a comfortable place to be; in fact, it's frightening. You see what's happening and worry you'll be tipped over and drowned by the storm. Right now, if you are unemployed, it probably feels like you're in the middle of a big storm and worried that it's all over for you, you'll never find another job.

The story continues, *Shortly before dawn Jesus went out to them, walking on the lake.* I've read this scripture many times, but I admit I missed this key point which he highlighted for me, that during the *storms of life,* Jesus comes to us, just like he came to them. He comes to help. If we spend all our time looking at the storms swirling around us, not only will we become more afraid, *we'll miss seeing Jesus coming to help.*

He came to the disciples in a way they weren't expecting, walking on the water. He often sends us help in ways we least expect it, too. *When the disciples saw him walking on the lake, they were terrified. "It's a ghost," they said, and cried out in fear. But Jesus immediately said to them: "Take courage! It is I. Don't be afraid." "Lord, if it's you," Peter replied, "tell me to come to you on the water."*

He then invited Peter to join him, saying trust me and come be with me. *"Come," he said. Then Peter got down out of the boat, walked on the water and came toward Jesus.* This worked well until Peter lost his focus on Jesus. *But when he saw the wind, he was afraid and, beginning to sink, cried out, "Lord, save me!" Immediately Jesus reached out his hand and caught him. "You of little faith," he said, "why did you doubt?" And when they climbed into the boat, the wind died down. Then those who were in the boat worshiped him, saying, "Truly you are the Son of God."*

Jesus is reaching out to you right now to help. Stop looking around at all that scares you and focus on him, put your trust in him. Life will calm down. You will receive his peace.

EMBRACE THE OPPORTUNITY!

I REMEMBER A DEVOTION a coworker used once in a meeting; it started with a story about monkeys and golf. As I remember it, when the British colonized India, they built a golf course for recreation. As the story went, there was a unique challenge to playing the course. After hitting their drives, which sometimes landed in the fairway and sometimes the rough, golfers would walk to where their ball was supposed to be, but it wouldn't be where it originally landed. Monkeys would come down out of the trees bordering the golf course, pick up the golf balls, and throw them. A ball in the rough might end up in the fairway. A ball in the fairway might end up behind the spot it had landed or ahead of it. I imagine the monkeys enjoyed watching the golfers getting frustrated.

They tried different things to get rid of the monkeys, but nothing worked. Finally, the golfers adopted a local rule agreeing to play the ball wherever the monkey dropped it. Some days a golfer might greatly benefit from the monkeys, others not. What changed was their *attitude*. They just accepted it would happen and moved on. To be successful on the course, I imagine you had to embrace the challenge and say, "How well can I benefit from this bad break?"

Hear these words from Psalm 26:2, *Test me, Lord, and try me, examine my heart and my mind.* This journey through a time of unemployment is a test for us. God wants to see how we respond, what we will do moving forward. Where do we place our trust? In ourselves and our abilities, or in him?

Too often in life, we try to make everything "perfect" and when we do, our frustrations increase because we're trying to make perfect what can't be made perfect. Right now, the monkeys have thrown your golf ball (your life) somewhere you didn't expect. They certainly did for me. The question is what we will do about it? Will we "whine," "cry," "gripe," "complain," "be angry," etc. about what happened? If so, what will it change? Nothing. In the end, we are still unemployed.

Instead, can we embrace what's happened? Can we learn to enjoy this opportunity? Can we figure out how to make this the best experience possible, even though it's not what we wanted? The answer is "Yes!" We can. I believe it's what God wants for us. I'm not saying it will be easy, but let's be positive about this and move forward.

When you talk with others about what's happened, share what's positive about what you are experiencing. Smile when you say it. Sometimes you might feel like you're faking it, but the more you say it, the more you'll believe it.

Embrace the journey and have some fun!

ONE DAY AT A TIME

I'M A PLANNER BY nature, one who likes to organize and prepare for whatever I'll be doing at home or at work. I wish I knew where this characteristic came from, but I really don't. We planners, like to know that everything is in order and the details are covered. I don't do idle time or unplanned time well, unless I've "planned" for it. I know, you're laughing at that statement along with my family. I don't like surprises much either, especially at work. Based on what you've learned about me, you probably know that I don't necessarily "roll with the punches" very well.

To give you an even better picture of me, let me share a personal story. Our family made a trip to San Diego where we visited Sea World. We were having a wonderful time and were at the dolphin tank where the dolphins swim up to the edge, so you can pet them. As I watched, I tired of waiting for the dolphin to swim over to where my wife and kids were. I unconsciously began to snap my fingers and motion for the dolphin to swim over to us. I didn't even realize what I was doing, but the rest of the family did and just started laughing. It was truly ridiculous to try to get dolphins to obey my snaps, but that's me. Maybe you can relate because you too are a planner or maybe you are married to one or know someone like me very well.

Now put yourself in my shoes and imagine me in a period of unemployment. Oh, my goodness! I couldn't see the future and didn't know when I'd have a new job. I couldn't control the process and it made me very uncomfortable. But what did I learn? I learned that there is a joy in living one day at a time. I also realized that's exactly what God wants us to do. To live one day at a time, thankful for that day and trusting him for our needs. In Matthew 6:9-13 we find the Lord's prayer. I'd like to highlight verse 11, where Jesus doesn't say our yearly, quarterly or even monthly bread; he says "daily" bread. *This, then, is how you should pray: "Our Father in heaven, hallowed be your name, your kingdom come, your will be done, on earth as it is in heaven. Give us today our daily bread. And forgive us our debts, as we also have forgiven our debtors. And lead us not into temptation; but deliver us from the evil one."*

I've learned to enjoy—or maybe I should say I was at least comfortable with—not knowing what was next. In doing so, I let God do the planning because while I'm a very good planner, he's ten times better than I could ever be. I began to experience things I never expected and had some real fun. As an example, an old friend called who knew I was out of work and wanted me to do some management training on a subject where I had some expertise. I did the training, had fun doing it, and the experience restored some self-confidence, something God knew I needed.

God knows what we need each day; just trust in him to provide it.

BUT I'M STILL ANGRY

I'M STILL ANGRY. ANGER isn't easy to get rid of and it doesn't just go away because we want it to go away. Acting like you aren't angry won't work because it will come back to you later. I know, because it did for me. I tried to put a positive spin on things as I spoke to others. "Yes, I lost my job, but it's okay. I'm not angry, I'm not bitter. I'll just move on." I almost fooled myself for a while. But then, the longer I was out of work, the angrier I became. I want to share some insights I've learned that might be helpful to you in dealing with your anger.

Writing is an excellent means for getting your anger out. A close friend of mine, Lynn, gave me a blank journal when I lost my job. At first, I didn't do anything with it; it just sat on my nightstand. Then one night I began to write. It became my own personal diary. I could write whatever I wanted in my journal. I wrote in it most days, and many of the devotions in this book came from looking back over the emotions I wrote about. Writing is therapeutic; it helps to get your emotions out, especially that anger. I recommend getting a journal and writing for yourself. In journaling, you can express thoughts that are hard to say, but on paper they don't go anywhere. You can be as angry, nasty, hurt, despondent, etc., as you want to be. Your journal isn't for others to read unless you want them to.

Another way to move your anger out is through help from others. In Ecclesiastes chapter 4, we are reminded that two are always better than one in dealing with problems. *Two are better than one, because they have a good return for their labor: If either of them falls down, one can help the other up. But pity anyone who falls and has no one to help them up. Also, if two lie down together, they will keep warm. But how can one keep warm alone? Though one may be overpowered, two can defend themselves. A cord of three strands is not quickly broken* (Ecclesiastes 4:9-12).

Talk about your anger to someone close to you. It could be your spouse or a close friend. One thing to keep in mind, however, is the challenge they'll have in remaining objective. Because they care for you, they might be too close to be helpful.

Another possibility is to visit with a professional psychologist. I met with a psychologist for a couple of months and it was well worth the money spent. There are a number of reasons to consider seeing a professional: 1) They are trained to help and will be better at getting to the heart of the issues and helping you sort them out. 2) They are objective; they aren't trying to please you or tell you what you want to hear. 3) You can say things to them that you might not say to others. They provide a completely safe place to talk.

Write it out, talk it out, and cry out to God. Just work to get your anger out and get past it.

A DIFFERENT RHYTHM
TO YOUR DAY

WHAT DO I DO with myself all day? For many years I knew what each day would bring, I woke up in the morning and went to work. Now all of that has changed and I don't have a schedule. I'm supposed to look for a job, but how much time will I spend on the search? I have this rare chance to do things that I've wanted to do but lacked the time. Can I really do them? How do I do both without guilt?

I wrestled with that issue of guilt for some time. If I was in my "job search" mode where I was networking or searching the Internet or calling folks, I felt guilty not being with my wife or children if they were available to do something. After all, I normally couldn't spend time with them, but now I could, so shouldn't I be with them? Then, if I was having fun with them, I felt guilty not working at finding a job because I needed to go back to work. I felt guilty all the time and didn't seem to have much peace.

Something I learned in the process of being unemployed is that there really are *no rules to this game*. I kept looking for the rulebook to tell me what I should be doing and could never find one. That's because we're each uniquely created by God and have our own set of personal circumstances. While everyone has opinions on what you should be doing, it's your life and you must live it. Their opinions are based upon their life. I found two keys to having any kind of personal peace.

I'm a "Type A" personality, always driving, always achieving, often in control or attempting to control the situation. It's especially tough for people like me because we think we control more than we do; but control is an illusion. The challenge is in letting go. Consider Jeremiah 10:23 *I know, O Lord, that a man's life is not his own; it is not for man to direct his steps.* This Scripture reminds me that if I want peace, I need to give up the very control that I desire. I've learned that the more I trust God and stop trying to do it all myself, the more I am at peace.

Your life will have a different rhythm and that's okay. When I reflect on my job search time, my best days were those when I was at peace, trusting that God had this all taken care of. On those days, I wasn't looking to the future, fretting or worrying about it. *May the God of hope fill you with all joy and peace as you trust in him, so that you may overflow with hope by the power of the Holy Spirit* (Romans 15:13).

My prayer is that you too will let go of your desire to control things and put your trust in God so that you might experience that special peace the world cannot understand.

FEAR AND WORRY

FEARS ... WE ALL have them and now you might have more than you've ever had before. I once saw an acronym for what "fear" stands for that made a lot of sense to me. I'd like to share it with you:

False
Evidence
Appearing
Real

I don't know what fears you are dealing with, but some that are relatively common for individuals in our situation might include, "I won't be able to find another good job"; "I won't make as much money as I used to make"; "We'll lose our house"; "We'll have to relocate away from family"; or _____ (you fill in the blank). We perceive these situations to be real and begin to fret and worry about them even though they haven't happened. Remember, if it hasn't happened, *it's not real*; it just appears to be real. And I'll bet most of your fears and mine haven't happened.

The words of Jesus about worry in Luke 12:22-34 are worth reading: *Therefore I tell you, do not worry about your life, what you will eat; or about your body, what you will wear. For life is more than food, and the body more than clothes. Consider the ravens: They do not sow or reap, they have no storeroom or barn; yet God feeds them. And how much more valuable you are than birds!* **Who of you by worrying can add a single hour to your life? Since you cannot do this very little thing, why do you worry about the rest?** *Consider how the wild flowers grow. They do not labor or spin. Yet I tell you, not even Solomon in all his splendor was dressed like one of these. If that is how God clothes the grass of the field, which is here today, and tomorrow is thrown into the fire, how much more will he clothe you—you of little faith! And do not set your heart on what you will eat or drink; do not worry about it. For the pagan world runs after all such things, and your Father knows that you need them. But seek his kingdom, and these things will be given to you as well. Do not be afraid, little flock, for your Father has been pleased to give you the kingdom.*

Focus on what Jesus is telling us: "don't worry," our Heavenly Father has everything taken care of—the little stuff and the big things. We can worry all we want, but it won't add a single hour to our lives. And if we can't add more time to our lives, then we certainly don't control anything of significance. All of that is under God's control.

USING YOUR TIME WELL

DURING MY JOURNEY, I had more free time than I was used to having. I suspect you do, too. Free time and the freedom to do things differently can be a blessing, but it can also be a serious challenge. According to a report by the National Institute for Health on College Drinking, the first six weeks of the freshman year are a vulnerable time for heavy drinking and alcohol-related consequences. Why is this? These freshmen have more unstructured time and freedom than they've ever had before and, unfortunately, they make bad choices. Consider yourself a freshman in college again, with some "dos" and "don'ts" for avoiding some painful mistakes.

Let's start with the "don'ts." If you drink alcohol, keep it at a moderate level and don't drink just because you have nothing else to do. If you watch TV from time to time, don't watch so much that you begin to know all the shows, what time they're on, etc.

What should you do with your extra time beyond searching for a job? Start by feeding your mind in a positive way. If you aren't already in the habit, spend some time each day in prayer and reading devotions or Scripture. God wants you to be close to him and the more you are in his Word, the closer you'll be.

I found it helpful to listen with regularity to inspirational podcasts from John O'Leary, a nationally recognized speaker from St. Louis. At the age of nine, John suffered third-degree burns on 100% of his body because of an accident. He wasn't given much chance to survive, but he did and today he offers inspiration to others for overcoming tragedies and living an inspired life. On a weekly basis he interviews a different person who has overcome some challenge. You'll find the interviews on his website; just search for "John O'Leary Inspires." They are great for my mind; the more positive inspiration we feed our minds, the better off we'll be.

Finally, do good things for others, even when we ourselves are suffering: *So then, those who suffer according to God's will should commit themselves to their faithful Creator and continue to do good* (1 Peter 4:19). If I'm not already doing that, when I'm suffering is a great time to start.

Look around and you'll see others who need help. Consider how you might have the time and ability to serve their needs. *Do not withhold good from those to whom it is due, when it is in your power to act. Do not say to your neighbor, "Come back tomorrow and I'll give it to you"—when you already have it with you* (Proverbs 3:27-28).

The Scriptures remind us not to say, "I'm too busy with my job search; I don't have time." Take the time to help others and do good.

SOWING SEEDS FOR THE FUTURE: NETWORKING PART 1

LET'S DIG INTO WHAT "networking" is as it relates to your job search and why it's important. In Part 2, I'll cover some tips on getting started in the process.

What do networks have to do with your job search? Everything! Each of us has a network of relationships through the people we know, and the more people looking out for potential job opportunities on your behalf, the better off you'll be. Additionally, some jobs don't get publicized where you can easily locate them. They're often part of the "hidden" job market, the type you learn about by "word of mouth." You'll want to use the relationships you already have for help in your job search and expand your network. It isn't just about meeting more people, though; it's about the quality of these relationships.

I encourage you to use this time to network with others as much as is possible and to consider it one of the most important methods for finding your next job. It means you'll be meeting with people, *face to face*, for breakfast, lunch, a "cup of coffee," drinks at the end of the day, or a visit to their office. The purpose of your time together is to learn more about them and share about yourself, your gifts, and especially what types of jobs you are looking for. If you already know the person, you'll enrich your relationship. If you don't know him or her, you're building a new relationship. I've found that people want to help, but they need to know that you're looking *and* what you're looking for.

In Matthew 13:3-8 we find a parable about sowing seeds. While Jesus is talking about sowing the seeds of God's word, I see applications to networking. *Then [Jesus] told them many things in parables, saying, "A farmer went out to sow his seed. As he was scattering the seed, some fell along the path, and the birds came and ate it up. Some fell on rocky places, where it did not have much soil. It sprang up quickly, because the soil was shallow. But when the sun came up, the plants were scorched, and they withered because they had no root. Other seed fell among thorns, which grew up and choked the plants. Still other seed fell on good soil, where it produced a crop—a hundred, sixty or thirty times what was sown."*

You'll meet with many people where nothing will come out of that meeting, or at least, not that you know of. In that case, what you shared fell on rocky soil. Others will like you and be interested in you but will have nothing open and don't know of anyone else who does. Consider these the seeds planted on shallow soil or among the weeds. But some of those you meet will know of an opening, introduce you to someone or pass your resume along to someone else who has an opening. That's the fertile soil.

I've spoken with many who have shared their stories of success through networking. It works. Get ready to start sowing seeds for your future.

SOWING SEEDS FOR THE FUTURE: NETWORKING PART 2

IN THE PREVIOUS DEVOTION, we learned what networking is. Now let's look at tips for getting started.

It's possible that the thought of networking makes you uncomfortable. You might be thinking "No one is going to want to talk with me" or "They won't listen or care what I have to say." Look at these excerpts from Exodus as God talks with Moses in front of the burning bush. I think you may find you have something in common with Moses. From Exodus 3:11-12, *Moses said to God, "Who am I that I should go to Pharaoh and bring the Israelites out of Egypt?" And God said, "I will be with you."* From Exodus 4:10-12, *[Moses said], "Pardon your servant, Lord. I have never been eloquent, neither in the past nor since you have spoken to your servant. I am slow of speech and tongue." The Lord said to him, "Who gave human beings their mouths? Who makes them deaf or mute? Who gives them sight or makes them blind? Is it not I, the Lord? Now go; I will help you speak and will teach you what to say."*

Sound familiar? Who am I that they will listen? What if they don't listen? I'm not a good speaker. The truth about this is that God will open the doors for people to take your calls and meet with you; God will give you the words to say. You don't need to worry about it.

Make a list of the friends and business associates you know well, because it's easier to meet with those you know. Start with those on your list who have connections to others in the business world. Call or email requesting a time to meet and let them know you're out of work and in the process of networking. Schedule your time around when and where it works best for the person you're meeting rather than asking them to adjust their schedule around yours.

When you meet, begin by thanking them for their time. Small talk is okay for getting started, especially if you already know them. Catch up, then share what you've been doing, the gifts you have, and the type of job you are looking for. If you know of specific companies you'd like to work for, tell them. Make sure you have a resume to give to them in case they learn of an opening that would be a good match for you. You should also ask if they know of someone who might be beneficial for you to meet, especially in a company of interest to you. If they do, ask them for an introduction, which will make it easier for you. Ask if there is anything you can do for them. Thank them again for their time.

Congratulations! You just networked. Don't forget to write a personal thank-you note and place it in the mail within two days. Gratitude is important in this process.

LET IT GO

WHEN YOU HEAR THE phrase "let it go," you just might hear the song from the movie *Frozen* playing in your head, especially if you've heard it often because you have a young daughter at home. On this journey, you need to continue to play that phrase over and over in your head, because it's something you need to do, even though doing so isn't easy. Or at least it wasn't easy for me. Sometimes I even felt "frozen." Even though I knew I couldn't solve this on my own, I kept trying to do so. I couldn't just "let it go" and give it to God; instead I held on tight. I was trying to "be God," instead of letting God be God *for me.*

As I was beginning to write these devotions, I looked at the many verses highlighted in my Bible, looking for ones that I might use. As I looked at each one, I noticed a consistent message throughout: Give it all to God and trust him. I won't share all the verses, but here are some worth reading time and again.

This is what the Lord says: **"Cursed is the one who trusts in man,** *who draws strength from mere flesh and whose heart turns away from the Lord. That person will be like a bush in the wastelands; they will not see prosperity when it comes. They will dwell in the parched places of the desert, in a salt land where no one lives. But blessed is the one who trusts in the Lord, whose confidence is in him. They* *will be like a tree planted by the water that sends out its roots by the stream. It does not fear when heat comes; its leaves are always green. It has no worries in a year of drought and never fails to bear fruit"* (Jeremiah 17:5-8). I felt "cursed" with a heavy load weighing me down. I didn't realize that by trusting in myself, I was bringing the "cursed" feeling upon me.

The Lord is good, a refuge in times of trouble. He cares for those who trust in him (Nahum 1:7). You feel honored when someone trusts you, and you don't want to let them down. I know that when people put their trust in me, I go the "extra mile" to make certain it works out and that I do what I say I'll do. God does that with us. He cares for us and loves us and won't let us down. He wants us to keep trusting in him for everything because it draws us closer to him.

The Lord is my strength and my shield; my heart trusts in him, and he helps me (Psalm 28:7). It's simple; when our hearts trust him, he helps us. My head so wanted to trust, but my heart just couldn't let go. Pretty stupid actually; but it happened. That was me. Life became so much easier when my heart let it go and trusted him.

If you're struggling, holding on tight, trying to figure this out all on your own, listen to that song and begin to "let it go!" Then take the big step—like the one off a diving board for the first time. Let go and trust. Once you do, you'll be much more content and at peace with what's happening in your life.

HUMBLE YOURSELF

WE ALL HAVE SOME amount of personal pride, or you might choose to call it self-confidence. Some individuals have more pride or self-confidence than others. Confidence comes from being successful. The more success you have, the more confident you will become. My self-confidence was shaken on this journey; I was humbled.

Why? Because I was used to being "successful" in my work. I had the answers to people's questions, which made me useful and helpful to others. I expect you did too. People you worked with knew what you did well, and they came to you for help. I was confident that every two weeks I would receive my paycheck and have money to do things. But this journey is different. I lost my job, my status among my peers or within the organization, and my paycheck. I became unimportant quickly. I learned I can influence parts of the search process, but I don't control the outcome. I can't make a job appear. I can't make someone hire me. Neither can you.

I believe a secret to success on this journey is the ability to be humble. You can't do this alone; you need help, from God and from others. You'll need to *ask for assistance*, and that might not be easy for you. Asking for assistance is a humbling experience because we are admitting "I don't have all the answers," "I can't do this on my own," and "I need others." But it's good for us to seek assistance. Don't let your personal pride get in your way.

On my journey, I got comfortable asking others I knew and didn't know for help. The more you do it, the easier it becomes. I had the opportunity to meet with several individuals who had started their careers working for me and now each of them was very successful in their profession. It was an interesting dynamic because I had once been their teacher helping them. I had been in the "power position" as their supervisor, but now I needed their help. I could have avoided asking them for help, but that would have been stupid. Not surprisingly, it was a wonderful experience. Each of them willingly gave of their time to meet with me. The conversations were great, and it gave me a chance to catch up with people I'd enjoyed working with and have immense respect for. I certainly know why they became successful.

But he gives us more grace. That is why Scripture says, "God opposes the proud but shows favor to the humble." Submit yourselves, then, to God. … Come near to God and he will come near to you. (James 4:6-8).

Humble yourself before God and others. Admit you don't have all the answers and that you need help. Trust that God will open those difficult doors.

DON'T WHINE

HOW YOU REACT TO the challenges you face and the journey you are now on says a lot about you. Others are watching you, making a mental note of what they see. What they don't want to see is for you to become a "whiner."

"Whiners" are always telling their problems to anyone who will listen. They're usually not very positive people. If you read *Winnie the Pooh* when you were young or to your children, you might remember Eeyore. Eeyore was a "whiner," an "oh woe is me" type of person. Contrast him with Tigger, who was always full of energy, happy, and upbeat. People can lose respect for "whiners" and usually avoid them if possible. So, if you have turned into a "whiner," the chances of anyone recommending you for a job can sharply diminish.

There is an organization in the St. Louis area called Executive Connections, which supports executives who are out of work and looking for their next job. One of their guiding principles jumped out at me: a "no whiners" rule. Here it is:

We believe in the No Whiners Rule. **We do not talk disparagingly about previous employers or colleagues.** *New members of Executive Connections must demonstrate that they are over any anxiety from their job loss and are prepared to begin their search with the spirit,* *enthusiasm and dedication that it requires.*

I bolded what I believe is the most important part of this principle, good advice for anyone who is in between jobs. Guard what you say to others about where you worked and keep it positive. If all you do is talk negatively, people will begin to question why you continued working for the company as long as you did.

I appreciate what the psalmist is saying in Psalm 141 about putting a guard over my mouth to keep me from being drawn into saying or doing bad things. *Set a guard over my mouth, Lord; keep watch over the door of my lips. Do not let my heart be drawn to what is evil so that I take part in wicked deeds along with those who are evildoers; do not let me eat their delicacies* (Psalm 141:3-4).

My prayer for you is that you resist the temptation to "whine" about your troubles and strive to remain positive in what you say to others. It will say more about you than you can imagine.

SHAKING THE DUST OFF YOUR FEET AND MOVING ON

WHAT WORLD ARE YOU living in today? Are you in the past, the present, or the future today? I found that I was often stuck living in the past, back at my old place of employment. How about you, are you still at your job?

I was talking to my good friend Lynn, a consultant I've worked with for many years, and he said, "I've got a great scripture for you." He looked up the verse on a note he'd made for himself and said it was Mark 6:11. *And if any place will not welcome you or listen to you, leave that place and shake the dust off your feet as a testimony against them.*

Such simple advice. So why was Jesus saying this to his disciples? He knew that when the disciples entered a town and began to preach, there would be times when people wouldn't listen. When this happened, they would have two choices: either work extra hard and *maybe* if they stayed with it long enough, *maybe,* just *maybe*, the people would begin to listen; or go elsewhere. Jesus didn't want them wasting their time on people who weren't going to change; he wanted them to move forward with their important work. He knew that time spent trying to change people who won't change was wasteful and would keep them from their goals. So, they were told to shake the dust off their feet and leave.

That was good advice for me, and maybe for you, too. Nothing I could do or say was going to change the decision that had been made regarding my job. It was already gone. Every moment I spent emotionally connected to that place of employment was keeping me from moving on. It was time to say to myself, "Dale, they don't know what they had in you. It will be their loss that you aren't there. You are so gifted, someone is going to be really lucky to get you at their company." Everything didn't magically change when I said it to myself—unfortunately, I needed to say it more than once, but after doing it a few times, it helped in moving me forward.

Once I moved out of the past, I moved into the present. The present is where God wants me to be and where he wants you to be. In the present, we're only focused on him; we aren't living in the past or worrying about the future. It's just him and us. My best days are ones where I stay in the present and I'm at peace.

I encourage you to take some time to "shake the dust off your feet" and to "kiss your old job goodbye." Give yourself a pep talk, reminding yourself of how gifted you are and what they're missing not having you there.

Then move into the present and experience the peace only God can bring.

WHERE'S MY SCHEDULE? FOCUS DAYS

MANY PEOPLE WILL SAY that you need to work as many hours finding a new job as you did working your previous job. If you had a full-time position, that probably means you'd be spending somewhere between 40-60 hours a week looking for a job. The challenge with this belief is there aren't enough things you can do in 40-60 hours to find a job. You don't control what prospective employers do and you can't control how quickly someone will respond to you. So how do you deal with the struggle of finding a new rhythm that works for you?

First, you need to give yourself permission to operate differently than before. The reality is there are no rules in this process. A good friend gave me a tip on how he handles his own schedule as someone in business for himself, which I then used in the search process. It helped me, and it might help you too.

A week has three types of days. The first type of day is a "focus" day. On these days you are focusing 100% on your job search. You focus on the tasks that are important to the search. You make phone calls, send emails, apply online for jobs, set up networking appointments, tweak your resume, meet with people, etc. You do whatever you need to do. It's a full day of effort, maybe eight or more hours. On these days, you put your personal life on hold, except in emergencies. Much like what we find referenced in Colossians 3:23. *Whatever you do, work at it with all your heart, as working for the Lord, not for human masters.*

Resist the temptation of doing what many do. They work at finding a job, but not very hard. They give up quickly or think that "God will find the job for me." Yes, we turn the control over to God, but he is watching to see what we do. Remember the Children of Israel after leaving Egypt? They wandered for 40 years until he had their attention and focus. I want you to give God your very best on these days. Keep the TV off. There are two verses in the book of Proverbs related to the type of effort God wants from us that are relevant to you for a focus type of day.

Those who work their land will have abundant food, but those who chase fantasies have no sense (Proverbs 12:11).

All hard work brings a profit, but mere talk leads only to poverty (Proverbs 14:23).

Even as you trust God to lead, he wants you to work hard on these days, to focus your energy on finding a new job, not just talk about working hard. Don't take the day off, focus.

WHERE IS MY SCHEDULE?
FLEX DAYS

NOW THAT WE'VE LOOKED at "focus" days where our primary purpose was focusing on the job search, let's zero in on "flex" days. This is the type of day where you spend time on the job search, but you aren't as focused; you can be open to changes to your schedule. These are days of both work and pleasure, which to most of us won't seem normal. We're used to doing one or the other.

What does a "flex" day look like? You'll plan to do work on your job search on these days, e.g., schedule appointments for meeting people, follow up on job leads, make calls, etc. On these days though, your schedule will be a little lighter. You might encounter a day where someone you wanted to meet with couldn't. So, if the weather is good, you might go to the park by yourself, with your spouse, or maybe your children or grandchildren. Or if someone calls and asks if you can play golf on a certain day or take a bicycle ride, you'll look at your schedule and if there aren't any appointments, you say yes and enjoy a round of golf or take that bicycle ride. The best part is you won't feel guilty because it was a "flex" day.

"Flex" days are a mixture of job search and fun. Is this biblical, you might ask? Yes, it is. If you search Scripture, you'll find that Jesus mixed rest and work in the same day many times. We need rest to prepare for the work ahead and we need rest to recharge after work.

In Matthew, Jesus was resting when a large crowd gathered. He wasn't ready to work yet so he gave himself permission to continue resting while going out in a boat to get away from the crowd. When he was rested and ready, he came in and preached a full day of parables: *That same day Jesus went out of the house and sat by the lake. Such large crowds gathered around him that he got into a boat and sat in it, while all the people stood on the shore. Then he told them many things in parables, saying: "A farmer went out to sow his seed ..."* (Matthew 13:1-3).

In the book of Mark, chapter 6, he fed 5,000 people. What did he do after expending a lot of energy? He rested. *Immediately Jesus made his disciples get into the boat and go on ahead of him to Bethsaida, while he dismissed the crowd. After leaving them, he went up on a mountainside to pray* (Mark 6:45-46).

Be flexible on your "flex" days. Take the day as it comes. On some flex days, you'll work more than you play. On others you'll play more than you work. Both are okay. Give yourself permission to enjoy them.

WHERE'S MY SCHEDULE? DAYS OFF

THE PREVIOUS TWO DEVOTIONS talked about "focus" days and "flex" days. The third type of day in a week is your "day off" from your job search. You took days off when you had a job and you should take them when you're searching for one.

Unless there's an emergency, your "day off" is an intentional day for rest from the search. How you use that day is up to you. For some, it'll mean play. Golf is my "mistress" in life, so if the weather is good, I like to play golf. You might prefer to do projects around the house, e.g., fixing, painting, or remodeling. Or you might use those days to get away from the house and go to museums or shop, etc. It's your day to do what you want.

My wife reminded me that I wasn't taking any days off and she commented that it affected my personality and my ability to "let go" and let God handle things. Therein lies a big challenge, the more we work, the more we think we're controlling this process and we aren't.

Yes, we are working hard at this. But remember, even God rested after creating this world, which is far more difficult than finding a job. *Thus, the heavens and the earth were completed in all their vast array. By the seventh day God had finished the work he had been doing; so on the seventh day he rested from all his work* (Genesis 2:1-2).

While on this journey, we are all anxious to get back to work. But God wants us to rest so that we are ready for him to restore us in a new job. Probably the most well-known psalm is Psalm 23. Can you find the references to rest in the first verses? *The Lord is my shepherd; I shall not want. He makes me to lie down in green pastures; He leads me beside the still waters. He restores my soul* (Psalm 23:1-2 KJV). How many days in your schedule become "focus" days, or "flex" days or days "off" is up to you. You need to decide what you need. It might even change as you progress on your journey. The key is, when you structure your days in this manner, you give yourself permission to enjoy what you are doing.

And remember, God created and then he rested. So by all means, create your own schedule ... then rest and enjoy.

SPACE INVADERS

I CAME INTO THE kitchen one night and told my wife we were playing a game from our past, Space Invaders. It was one of the earliest video games you could play in the late 1970s. My wife remembered the game. My wife and I have been happily married for almost 40 years and we have a good relationship, but good relationships can get stressed too. She works part-time outside the home and her additional time is usually spent with our grandchildren. What a blessing for them and for her; I'm glad she does it.

But our life had become like Space Invaders. Our worlds were clashing, because we were both in each other's space and it was causing conflict between us. You may or may not be experiencing this same struggle; I wouldn't be surprised if you are.

While searching for a job, I'm home more than I've ever been before because our home has become my "office." I've entered her world, one I knew about but rarely saw. And my wife has entered mine.

I became frustrated with a lack of space and privacy in my "office," something that never happened when I worked. It seemed to me that she and the grandchildren were always around when I needed or wanted to work. This was a double stress for me because I loved having the grandchildren around, so I was always in a quandary of play or work? My wife would tell you that I was getting too involved in her world, asking too many questions and offering too many opinions on how she operated. Nothing intentional was done by either of us, it just happened. We each had unexpressed expectations and frustrations. We were both frustrated and stress increased.

Stress can affect how we talk to one another, so good communication is important. Colossians 3:19 has some great advice about "how" we should talk to one another. *Husbands, love your wives and **do not be harsh with them**.* I believe the text applies to both spouses in a marriage or both partners in a relationship. Don't speak harshly; it will help absolutely nothing.

When stress flares, you need to put the fire out. The sooner, the better. I recommend you have such a conversation over a meal and outside the home if possible so that it can be on neutral ground. Then share with each other from the heart—the good, the bad, and the other stuff that's happening. Stop reading "intent" into any part of the conversation as this puts obstacles in the way of coming to a resolution. You might even shed a few tears.

With listening, talking, and *working together* (you are, after all, a team), you'll get back on track and draw closer together.

HOW SHOULD I PRAY?

I PRAY REGULARLY AND always have. But these days, God and I are talking more often, which shouldn't be a surprise to anyone. When life is good, we often forget to say, "Thanks, God, for these gifts that make life good." I'm guilty of that; are you? When we're in trouble, we start yelling, "God, where are you? I need your help." I imagine you might also be talking to God more often as you go through this journey. I know he likes it when we talk regularly with him.

My challenge these days is that I'm a little uncertain as to how I should pray. What do I mean? It means I'm torn by what I should be asking God for. I want a job, which seems like a simple prayer; but how specific should I be? Should I be praying for a specific job, a specific company, or a specific position? Those are all things that have come to mind as I've prayed. I'm torn because I think if I get too specific, then it feels like I'm telling God that I have the answers to what is best for me. And I know that I don't. At the same time, I believe God wants to know what's on our heart and mind because he loves us and wants to help. It's a quandary for me.

Let me share something I learned from Scripture about prayer. In Mark 11:24 we read these words of Jesus: *Therefore I tell you, whatever you ask for in prayer, believe that you have received it, and it will be yours.* In this verse, we're told to pray expectantly; in other words, pray believing those results will happen. God wants us to be confident in him as our Heavenly Father, because he can deliver for us.

Then comes faith—we need to have faith in God. What is faith? It's defined for us in Hebrews 11:1. *Now faith is confidence in what we hope for and assurance about what we do not see.* Faith is assurance, even about those things we cannot see. These days, I can't see the future. Like you, I don't know what job will be next for me. I don't know where I'll work, what my title will be, what my pay will be. I know nothing. At the same time, I realized I know everything. God has this taken care of for me, and it will happen—in his time.

These two verses have shaped a basic prayer that I've prayed on this journey. I pray with confidence that I know he'll take care of me. Here it is. "God, I know you have a plan for me and that it will be wonderful. I trust and am confident it will happen, and I accept that I don't know when it will happen. I don't doubt that you'll take care of me. Give me patience as I wait for you to reveal your plan to me."

Pray confidently that God will take care of you; trust in him on this journey.

DON'T WORRY!

WHAT, ME WORRY? SURE, worry is part of life. For some, it's a constant part of daily life. They think, fret, and worry about the future. For others, it's situational. I admit that often I worry far more than I should. During this time of unemployment, "worry" will probably be with you daily. You may be able to put it out of your mind, but when you least expect it, it rears its ugly head and you worry. We're human after all and humans do worry.

There are so many things for us to worry about.

- Will I ever get a new job? Will it pay as much as I used to make?
- Will it be a step down from where I've been?
- Will I be successful again?
- How will we make it financially?
- What will my kids think?
- Will we need to relocate to a new city away from family?
- When will it ever end?

You can add your own specific worries to the list; but worrying will only wear you down as described in Proverbs 12:25. *Anxiety weighs down the heart, but a kind word cheers it up.* That describes it so very well. When we worry, our hearts are "heavy" and it becomes a burden too heavy to carry.

Worry does nothing positive for us; it only drains us. Think about the worries I listed or some of your own. Can you do anything to impact the outcome? No, because they are all "what ifs." They haven't happened. If you would ever talk with my friend Sally about your worries for the future, she'd remind you of what her mother always said, "You can choke on a cheese sandwich tomorrow and not be around to worry about it."

God has a plan for us when worry creeps into our lives. We find it in Philippians 4:6-7. *Do not be anxious about anything, but in every situation, by prayer and petition, with thanksgiving, present your requests to God. And the peace of God, which transcends all understanding, will guard your hearts and your minds in Christ Jesus.* God knows we'll be anxious about the future, but he says, "Don't be." And when we do worry, he wants us to talk to him! That's what prayer is, our conversation with God. Through prayer, God draws us closer to him. The closer we are to him, the better he can guard our hearts and minds, to keep them from wandering toward "worry" about what we can't control.

When worry creeps into your life, immediately start praying. Let God draw you closer to himself and watch those worries disappear.

AN ATTITUDE OF GRATITUDE

HAVE YOU THANKED GOD today for the *gift of this day*, this opportunity to be alive in his kingdom? You might be thinking, "What's there to be thankful for? I'm unemployed." True, but the Apostle Paul urges us to have an attitude of gratitude, being thankful in all circumstances. In 1 Thessalonians 5:16-18 we read, *Rejoice always, pray continually, give thanks in **all** circumstances; for this is God's will for you in Christ Jesus.*

Notice the word "all." He doesn't say give thanks for the good things when you get them; he says give thanks in "all" things. Even this period of unemployment is a blessing. Take time to list the blessings you have in your life right now—things like family, friends, health, skills, etc. Now list the challenges you face. Being unemployed is one of them, but what else? Now, which list is longer? I'd put money on your blessings list. Take a moment and give thanks to God for your blessings, as well as your challenges.

On this journey, you are receiving unexpected gifts, such as opportunities to be loved by others. Often, we just accept gifts as if they were supposed to happen, like the ten lepers whom Jesus healed. Only 10% came back to say thanks. *Now on his way to Jerusalem, Jesus traveled along the border between Samaria and*

Galilee. As he was going into a village, ten men who had leprosy met him. They stood at a distance and called out in a loud voice, "Jesus, Master, have pity on us!" When he saw them, he said, "Go, show yourselves to the priests." And as they went, they were cleansed. One of them, when he saw he was healed, came back, praising God in a loud voice. He threw himself at Jesus' feet and thanked him—and he was a Samaritan. Jesus asked, "Were not all ten cleansed? Where are the other nine? Has no one returned to give praise to God except this foreigner?" Then he said to him, "Rise and go; your faith has made you well" (Luke 17:11-19).

My question for you today is, do you say "thanks" upon receiving a special gift? Are you one of the 90% who said nothing or are you the 10% who say "thanks"?

When you meet with someone for networking, did you personally call or write a note of appreciation? I've discovered that writing a personal note is very meaningful. I can text, send an email, or post on Twitter in a matter of seconds, but it doesn't take much effort and it's not really a sign of sincerity. I encourage you to get into the habit of writing personal notes of gratitude. A personal note takes time and heart to do and people know that. It will be remembered.

An attitude of gratitude goes a long way. Most especially, say "thanks" to God for the many times he shows his amazing grace through others.

WHERE DID MY SELF-CONFIDENCE GO?

I'VE LOST SOMETHING ON this journey. It was just here; but now it's gone. It's my self-confidence and I want it back. I feel "adrift" these days, lacking confidence and direction. I don't like the feeling. What do I do?

Our self-confidence comes from being successful. When I was young and learning to tie my shoes, I didn't have much confidence in my skill. Once I learned it and repeated it successfully many times, I was totally confident that I could do it. It's true for all of us as we gain confidence with each success. When I had my job, I had confidence in my abilities to do it well, confidence that had been built over years of experience. Now that I'm unemployed, I'm not "doing" the things I used to do. The skills in looking for a new job are often different from the ones we used in our job. In many ways, we're starting over.

When I was employed, I also had direction. I knew what I needed to be working on; I didn't wonder if I was going to be paid and I assumed my job would be there if I did it well. Without a job, I don't feel like I have direction other than to find a new job.

I accept that the challenge I face—and maybe you too—is that *my confidence was in my own skills and abilities.* I'll admit, I took for granted what I had in my job. If someone asked, I would say that I knew it was a gift from God, but day to day, I too often believed it was really all about me and how good I was at my job.

To get our confidence back, you and I need to shift the source of our confidence. That's what we learn in Psalm 20:7. *Some trust in chariots and some in horses, but we trust in the name of the Lord our God.* Instead of believing in ourselves, we need to shift to a belief that our skills and abilities come from God. But shifting our confidence is easier said than done.

What we're up against in this job search feels like a monumental challenge. And it is. It's probably like nothing you've ever tackled before, it certainly is for me. When we're in as big a battle as this, we need help. We need to remember that the battle isn't ours alone, it's God's. Let's give it to him. *"Be strong and courageous. Do not be afraid or discouraged because of the king of Assyria and the vast army with him, for there is a greater power with us than with him. With him is only the arm of flesh, but with us is the Lord our God to help us and to fight our battles." And the people gained confidence from what Hezekiah the king of Judah said* (2 Chronicles 32:7-8).

When I give it over to God, he restores my confidence. And I want to remember always that my confidence is in him, not in me.

TAKE ME BACK TO EGYPT

MY JOB, LIKE MOST jobs, wasn't perfect. But there was much more good about it than bad. I knew what I was doing, liked who I worked with, and believed in the company. But was I really energized and was it what I really wanted to keep doing for a long time? If I'm honest, the answer is "no." But taking the initiative to make a change wasn't high on my list. I did look from time to time, but not an all-out campaign to find a different job.

Some people like the process of changing jobs because changing fits their personality. Others hate what they are doing or who they work for so badly they want to change. But for most of us, change means the unknown, and the unknown is frightening. We fear that if we make a change, it could be worse than what we have today. So we stay put. We might be unhappy and complain, but we know what to expect from one day to the next. We justify to ourselves that it's not perfect, but it's okay. But in not making a change, it's possible we miss out on something that could be so much better. We might experience more joy. We might even get paid more or have better benefits.

I wouldn't be surprised to learn that you wish you were back at your old job. It would be so much better than looking for a new one. The unknown is scary, but remember that you aren't alone. Think about the time the Children of Israel were escaping from the Egyptians and saw them coming after them: *As Pharaoh approached, the Israelites looked up, and there were the Egyptians, marching after them. They were terrified and cried out to the Lord. They said to Moses, "Was it because there were no graves in Egypt that you brought us to the desert to die? What have you done to us by bringing us out of Egypt? Didn't we say to you in Egypt, 'Leave us alone; let us serve the Egyptians'? It would have been better for us to serve the Egyptians than to die in the desert!"* (Exodus 14:10-12). Even after escaping slavery and misery, at the first sign of trouble, they wanted to go back.

You are making an Exodus right now, whether you planned it or not. You might spend time thinking about going back. You might even dream that it was a mistake and that they'll realize it and ask you to come back. Maybe you hope they'll pay you to come back as a consultant, or if you were laid off, you hope you'll be recalled. Just remember that God wants the very best for you—a life lived to the fullest as described in John 10:10 where Jesus says, *The thief comes only to steal and kill and destroy; I have come that they may have life and have it to the full.*

God can open so many doors, if we just trust. Don't spend time dreaming about your past. Dream of the wonders of God and all that he can do for you.

IT'S LIKE REPOTTING A PLANT

THERE IS A SPECIAL bond that exists between those who have lost their job. About 10 months after leaving my job at a large hospital, Donna reached out to me. Donna had been a manager at the same hospital and lost her job shortly after me. She wanted to talk with me because there was an opening where she was working, and she thought of me, wondering if I would be interested.

As we talked, she gave me all the details of the position, and then I asked her how she was doing in her new job. She became so excited telling me about her new job and how well it was going. It was easy to see that she had found happiness; she was experiencing more joy than she had in her previous job. She said she felt like a plant that had been repotted. She realized that she had grown about as much as she could where we had worked together, and now in her new environment, she was growing at a more rapid pace.

I'm not much of a gardener myself, so I would never have thought of that analogy. But it's a great one. My wife enjoys gardening and I've watched her nurse small plants into bigger ones by repotting them in a different pot or replanting them in a different spot where they will grow better. Left in too small a pot, the plant could never grow to its full potential.

I know that professionally, we also need growth opportunities, or we will grow stale. Maybe you had become stale in your position. Look at this opportunity as a chance to grow professionally and spiritually. Of the two, your spiritual growth is more important. It is my hope that through this process your faith will grow and for that you will feel thankful. *We ought always to thank God for you, brothers and sisters, and rightly so, because your faith is growing more and more, and the love all of you have for one another is increasing* (2 Thessalonians 1:3).

Remember, God provides all you need to grow. *Now he who supplies seed to the sower and bread for food will also supply and increase your store of seed and will enlarge the harvest of your righteousness* (2 Corinthians 9:10).

I pray that when you land in your new position, you'll see the fruits of your patience in the harvest.

WHERE DOES TRUST COME IN?

WHAT IS TRUST? I think the word itself is often misused. The dictionary definition contains some of the following, of which I've highlighted three words:

- Assured reliance on the character, ability, strength, or **truth** of someone or something;
- One in which **confidence** is placed;
- Dependence on something future: **hope**

Truth – If I trust someone, I can rely on them to always tell me the truth, whether I like it or want to hear it.

Confidence – If I trust someone, I have confidence that they will do what they say they'll do; I don't have to wonder if it will happen.

Hope – Anticipating the future and, as it relates to trust, knowing that it will happen.

Who do you trust these days? Like most people, I trust myself and have confidence in my abilities. I trust my wife, my family, and my close friends. I've also trusted many people I worked with. The people I trust live out truth, confidence, and hope for me.

Who don't you trust these days? Is it a long list? I wouldn't be surprised to find people where you previously worked on your list. How much do you trust God right now? What bothers me is that when I don't trust, I start doubting the people and things I used to have confidence in.

The journey you are on is all about trust. In some ways, it's a test. As much as I trust myself, my spouse, or family and friends, we are all human and we will fall short; we will fail. The following text from Jeremiah reminds us that trust in God will never let us down. *This is what the Lord says:* **"Cursed is the one who trusts in man,** *who draws strength from mere flesh and whose heart turns away from the Lord. That person will be like a bush in the wastelands; they will not see prosperity when it comes. They will dwell in the parched places of the desert, in a salt land where no one lives.* **But blessed is the one who trusts in the Lord, whose confidence is in him.** *They will be like a tree planted by the water that sends out its roots by the stream. It does not fear when heat comes; its leaves are always green. It has no worries in a year of drought and never fails to bear fruit"* (Jeremiah 17:5-8).

Put your trust in God and be amazed at the blessings that flow from him to you.

BE STILL AND KNOW THAT I AM GOD

IF YOU LIVE IN a large city like I do, you'll know that it can be noisy. When I was young, we often went out to the "country" with family and friends to go camping and/or fishing. I was always amazed at how quiet and still it was. The noises of the city simply weren't there. You could even talk in a normal voice and it sounded loud. It was easy to hear anything others said, no matter how far away they were. My dad often told us (my brothers and friends) that we were too loud, and we needed to be quiet, but often we weren't any louder than back at home. It sounded louder simply because it was so quiet.

Right now, you're on a journey full of anxiety and full of quiet. It's an odd combination, isn't it? I'm reminded of Psalm 46 and I hope you'll take the time to read the entire psalm. Listen to these words from verses 1-3: *God is our refuge and strength, an ever-present help in trouble. Therefore, we will not fear, though the earth give way and the mountains fall into the heart of the sea, though its waters roar and foam and the mountains quake with their surging.*

I like the phrase "ever-present help" found in verse 1. God is my lifeline all the time, whenever I'm in trouble. Right now, you may be thinking "I need help." The good news is that God is right there with you; you need not fear.

Look at how the psalmist describes God: *The Lord Almighty is with us; the God of Jacob is our fortress* (Psalm 46:7). Look up the word almighty in the dictionary and it will tell you the word means "having absolute power over all." The Lord Almighty. Think about it; he's on your team right now.

Verse 10 contains a short and simple phrase, one that helps me accept what's happening: *Be still and know that I am God!* There's probably more stillness and quiet in your life right now than you're probably used to and likely more than you want. I know it was that way for me. While I had always wished for more quiet time, when I lost my job I had too much.

So what do you do with the quiet? I propose taking time to listen to what God is telling you. Don't talk, just listen. He wants your complete and undivided attention, but he wants your trust, too. He wants you to stop looking around at what scares you and to trust in him—the Lord Almighty—to bring you to the next opportunity, a place where you will succeed.

In the stillness and the quiet you are experiencing, be aware of God's presence. The Lord Almighty is on your team. Relax and listen; he'll give you direction.

CONSIDER YOURSELF AN ARROW

STEPHANIE WORKED FOR ME for five years. She's a wonderfully talented young professional with a great future. When I left my job, I received a card from her with arrows on it. The personal note she wrote was meaningful, but the most impactful part of the card were the words about an arrow. Here's what it said:

AN ARROW CAN ONLY BE SHOT BY PULLING IT BACKWARD.

WHEN LIFE IS DRAGGING YOU BACK WITH DIFFICULTIES,
IT MEANS IT'S GOING TO LAUNCH YOU
INTO SOMETHING GREAT.

SO JUST FOCUS AND KEEP AIMING.

The analogy of the arrow is like the development process in life. You get stress before success. In the role of a leader, I look for potential in those who work for me that many times they don't see for themselves. Often they lack confidence. My job is to test, stretch, push, pull, affirm, and love them as part of their growth process. When I'm stretching them, I remain nearby as their "lifeline" to make certain they are okay, until they have the confidence to do it on their own. It's the development process. If everything were easy, there would be no growth. Think about it. Who helped you grow because they cared enough to push and stretch you?

Our Heavenly Father does that for us too. He sees the potential that often we don't see. He sees all that you and I can be in this world. How does he bring out the full potential in us? He allows stresses in our life to strengthen and prepare us for what's next. I've found that to be true all my life. Some of the most difficult challenges I've experienced have helped me for facing other challenges.

You're going through some serious stress right now. You are the arrow being pulled back and there is a great deal of tension in that process. You're getting ready to be launched to something special. In which direction are you being aimed? I don't know, but God does. Take Proverbs 3:5-6 to heart: *Trust in the Lord with all your heart and lean not on your own understanding; in all your ways submit to him, and he will make your paths straight.* There's the recipe for success in this Scripture.

Don't trust in yourself and what you know. It's not enough. You can't do this based on what you know no matter how good you are. We need to turn this problem over to God. Let him direct your path; he will open doors and select the right landing spot for you.

KEEPING OTHERS INFORMED

YOU'RE ON THIS JOURNEY you never thought you'd be on, unemployed and looking for a job. Progress is often slow, as the employment process takes time. You're doing all you can do and it's on your mind 24/7 because it's happening to you. But it isn't "top of mind" for everyone else. The reality is that for most people you know, their day-to-day life hasn't changed with your unemployment. They care about you, but life goes on for them.

My friends in the marketing profession remind me I need to be *"top of mind"* with others if I want them to continue helping me. When you first shared the news, you were "top of mind" for them. But with each day, it becomes less important in their world. Reminding them reengages them. If they know nothing, they'll be passive. You want people to be active to help you.

One of the challenges you face is keeping others informed about your search. Over the years I've met with a lot of people who were networking. Every time, I asked them to stay in contact with me, but most of them never reached out to me again. While I wanted to continue helping them, I didn't know if they still needed my help or if they had found a new job. I'm less engaged in helping them if I don't know what's going on.

What gets in your way when it comes to keeping people informed? I find it's often one of two things. First, we just don't think of it. We forget that their world didn't change the way ours did. The other common reason is personal pride. My pride was bruised when I became unemployed; as a result, the mere thought of reminding the world that I'm still unemployed is hard to do. It's as if I'm shouting, "Hey world, it's me, Dale, and guess what? I'm still unemployed. There's nothing wrong with me, but I still don't have a job. I just wanted you to know."

Personal pride stood in my way. Pride will bring us down, as described in Proverbs 29:23. *Pride brings a person low, but the lowly in spirit gain honor.* Even though it was difficult, I pushed away my personal pride and I reached out. I sent emails monthly to my friends and family who knew, as well as everyone I had networked with. I was amazed at the number of phone calls, emails, and texts I received thanking me for the update and recommitting to helping me out. Those calls, texts, and emails were also very affirming for me, they built me up. They were a reminder of how many were praying for me, of how many really cared. I felt better remembering I wasn't alone on this journey.

Even though you may not want to, I encourage you to send something out on at least a monthly basis. (See examples in Appendix D.) It's not easy, but it's important. In doing so, I believe you'll be blessed by the affirmation you receive from others.

YOUR STRENGTH IS YOUR WEAKNESS

I WAS HAVING LUNCH with one of my dearest friends, Cindy, who lives in Kansas City. We were enjoying some wonderful barbeque and I was talking about my recent job loss and what had happened. She said, "Dale, your strength is your weakness." I asked her to elaborate. She went on to say that in life we all have strengths, things we do well. We might think our strengths will always help us in life and especially in a work setting, but sometimes they don't. In fact, our strengths can work against us and become our weakness.

Those strengths may even have impacted why you don't have your job now.

As an example, you might be very good at always meeting your goals; you are an achiever. Does that make you the favorite person in your department? Probably not. Those who don't produce as well will feel inferior or be intimidated. So your strength might be a weakness in your relationships with peers.

You might be very good at holding people accountable for their work performance and their responsibilities. If you do, I doubt that those you hold accountable appreciate that quality. Don't be surprised if they spread rumors that you didn't "treat them well" because that deflects attention from their productivity. Your strength in holding people accountable can become a weakness for you.

This also happens with the devil, who is always around us. Remember what is said about the devil in 1 Peter 5: 8-11? *Be alert and of sober mind.* **Your enemy the devil prowls around like a roaring lion looking for someone to devour.** *Resist him, standing firm in the faith, because you know that the family of believers throughout the world is undergoing the same kind of sufferings. And the God of all grace, who called you to his eternal glory in Christ, after you have suffered a little while, will himself restore you and make you strong, firm and steadfast. To him be the power for ever and ever. Amen.*

The devil is always looking to mess with us, to take us "down a notch." He picks at our strengths, weaknesses, and fears. When I was out of work, he came at me. How about you? Do you sense he's around coming to get you?

One of my personal traits is "perfection" in my work. While I know it was never perfect, I worked hard to do it the best I could. Doing it "okay" wasn't good enough. I took pride in the results. But it's a weakness now that I'm unemployed because the devil says I don't have any value because I don't have any work to do. And at times, I believe him. Then I stop and remember that God controls everything—not me—and God loves me. In those tough times I need to say "be gone Satan" and trust God.

When you're tempted to believe the devil's lies, stand firm in your faith and tell him to "take a hike!"

I MISS WORKING

WHILE UNEMPLOYED, MY WIFE and I saw the movie *The Post* with Tom Hanks and Meryl Streep. A great movie; I loved it. But it also stirred in me some emotions about work. I realized I felt like I was on a team, but the coach had me on the bench. Who wants to sit on the bench? I want to be in the game. I miss being in the game; I miss working. Some people might say "you're crazy" because their job is ... well, it's work. It's what they do for money, not what they love doing. I've always been blessed to do what I loved and never considered it work. If you're like me, it's hard because you miss something you loved doing.

What do I miss about work? Many things. I miss the camaraderie of work, being part of something beyond myself. Working together toward a common goal. I miss the team I worked with, especially "my team." They were great, and I enjoyed them personally and professionally. I think it's normal that whenever we stop working, even if it's a planned retirement, we miss the people most.

I miss the energy of work, especially when there's a significant project or initiative of importance. Those efforts that bring out the best in people. Yes, there is often some stress, but stress isn't a totally bad thing.

I miss being important in my job, being needed. I don't mean that in a self-centered way, like "look at me, I'm important." No matter what your role, the organization you work for needs you. You are important. I miss being needed for something other than chores around the house.

God tells us that whatever we do, do it with our whole heart. *Whatever you do, work at it with all your heart, as working for the Lord, not for human masters, since you know that you will receive an inheritance from the Lord as a reward. It is the Lord Christ you are serving* (Colossians 3:23-24). I believe I did that, and I miss using the gifts God has given me to help others through my work.

I miss dressing up for work, caring what I look like. When I'm around the house, it doesn't matter what I look like, and I often succumb to dressing like every day is Saturday.

The good news is that this time of not working will end. You're storing up energy and learning more about what's most important for you in your next job. Soon you'll be "back in the game" and loving it.

THE LOTUS FLOWER

MY GOOD FRIEND JANE and I worked together for many years. She's one of the brightest, most creative, thoughtful, and insightful people I know. She always had a picture of a lotus flower in her office, but I never even noticed the uniqueness of the picture. Then I watched as she went through some difficult times working with and for people who were "passive-aggressive," e.g., individuals who never dealt directly with her about a problem but were always willing to talk to others. Those types of individuals are very insecure, but, unfortunately, they don't hurt themselves; they make life difficult for others. One day I was trying to encourage her as we talked about the challenges she faced. The picture of the lotus flower came up and she encouraged me.

If you aren't into plants or flowers, you might not know much about the lotus flower. I certainly didn't. What I learned is that it only blooms in the mud and the muck, which is not a pleasant environment at all. Jane told me the picture reminded her that in the middle of the "mud and muck" of life or work, we can still bloom and be beautiful. We don't have to be defined by our environment or the circumstances. It was an important lesson for me ... and for you too.

You might feel like you are in the "mud and muck" of life right now. Your "mud and muck" might be that you don't have a job and, yes, maybe you got the "short end of the stick" and weren't treated fairly. You feel uncertain about who you are now that you've lost your position. You're concerned about finances. This may have stressed a relationship.

Whatever the case, you have a choice to make about how you deal with it. You can be inwardly focused on the "crap" you're dealing with and be miserable. It's easy to do and there are plenty of people who will feel sorry for you. You can even have a "pity party" each day if you want. Or you can be a lotus flower and triumph over your circumstances. Remember what it says in Ecclesiastes 3:11, *[God] has made everything beautiful in its time.*

This can be your time, right now, to bloom and be beautiful despite the "mud and muck." Don't let this experience define you in a negative way. Rise above your circumstances. Be determined that you will flourish. Keep your focus on God, not your circumstances. Remember that God will meet every need as we turn everything over to him. Enjoy blooming!

I WENT MISSING

I WENT MISSING RECENTLY and I didn't know it happened. No, not physically, but mentally and emotionally. It impacts my wife when this happens and I'm sorry to say it does happen from time to time. Sometimes it's for a day; sometimes it's a couple of days. I get lost in myself and what's happening to me, my situation. The result is I'm not there emotionally.

I often don't realize that I've gone missing until she says something to me like "You're distant" or "Are you okay?" Sometimes I might argue that I'm just fine, but I ask myself, how did that happen? I thought I was in control of my emotions; I thought I was doing well. Usually, I know she's right and I apologize. Sometimes we talk and in doing so, I share what I've been going through. Talking is good, but sometimes even I don't know what made me distant.

You may be lucky and not have experienced this yet, but chances are good that you will. If you are a spouse, partner, or significant other reading this, just know that when it happens, it's not intentional. We don't intend to drift away.

Why do I think it happens? Perhaps because we get too "self-absorbed" in the process. We spend a lot of time by ourselves, planning and doing. But is that how we're supposed to live?

Above the altar at my home church are these words from Scripture: *And he died for all, that those who live **should no longer live for themselves** but for him who died for them and was raised again* (2 Corinthians 5:15).

As I reflect on this Scripture, I am reminded that my life is not supposed to be about me, it's about Jesus who loved others above himself. In response, we love and care for others.

This is also great protection against getting lost and becoming self-absorbed. There are many ways to do this; choose what works best for you. It could be just spending time with your children or grandchildren, time doing what they want to do. It could be time with your spouse, doing what he or she wants to do. It might be volunteering in your community or at a local charity. Just find some way to give of yourself to others.

Doing for others will also help you. It will occupy your time, something you have way too much of these days. It also keeps you from thinking too much about yourself and the challenges you face. Turn your focus from self to others, the sooner, the better.

BE YOUR OWN CADDIE

EVERYONE NEEDS A CADDIE, not just a golfer. If you don't golf, you might wonder what a caddie is. Professional golfers use them on a golf course to carry their bag to lighten their load. The caddie also gives advice to the player about distances, which club to use and hazards that are seen or unseen. But I believe the real value of having a caddie is the moral support. They encourage their golfers throughout the round, always saying positive things to them to keep their spirits up. Not surprisingly, if you have a positive attitude, you'll play better.

We need a caddie in life too. If you're married, hopefully your spouse serves as your caddie, your cheerleader, the person who will say positive things to you, especially on this journey. I'm so blessed that my wife, Deb, does this well for me. Or maybe you have someone—a girlfriend or boyfriend, partner, close friend, or family member—who serves as your caddie. Don't underestimate their importance. You'll need that encouragement.

But you also need to be your own caddie, to believe in yourself. Remind yourself how good you are. It's easy to forget—especially now—that God created us: *For you created my inmost being; you knit me together in my mother's womb* (Psalm 139:13). And if you don't know this already then listen very carefully, you are amazingly and wonderfully made. In Psalm 17:8 the psalmist says we are the "apple of his eye": *Keep me as the apple of your eye.* Best of all, he loved each of us so much that he died for us: *Greater love has no one than this: to lay down one's life for one's friends* (John 15:13). Can you be loved any more than that? I don't think so.

Dr. Bob Rotella is a sports psychologist. In his book *The Unstoppable Golfer* he wrote about the importance of self-image, what we think of ourselves and the impact on positive performance. He writes *"Try to understand first that you are what you have thought of yourself and you will become what you think of yourself from this moment onward."* He goes on to say, *"Your brain is a faithful servant. On some level it remembers all the things you think about yourself."* What do you say to yourself about you?

When your caddie notices you are down, he or she might give you a pep talk, but that person isn't around all the time. Every day, you need to be your own caddie. Fill your head with positive thoughts. Nothing negative. Remind yourself how good you are. Say positive things like "Some company is going to be lucky to get me," or "If they didn't want me, they are really missing out." Remind yourself, "God has something awesome in store for me; I can't wait to see what it is."

God created you; he loves you; he wants nothing but the best for you.

TIME USED TO PASS SO QUICKLY

WHAT A DIFFERENCE WE experience in the "pace of life" when we're out of a job. Time used to pass so quickly while immersed in work. It was Monday, then in the blink of an eye, it was Friday. It was the month of May and summer was starting in another blink of an eye, it was August and summer was over.

Now your pace has slowed down, and you may find yourself thinking, "It's killing me." But has life really slowed down? One reason every day seems long and the weeks seem to take forever is that you've lost your "work" routine, which brought a certain rhythm to your life. You got up at a similar time each day, commuted to work in a similar manner, you parked in a similar spot and did whatever it was that you did at work. Time passes more quickly when we have a routine. But now you have no work routine to pass the time. You're probably trying to find ways to "keep busy." I'll bet some projects around the house are even getting done. I know they did at my house. I even tried to clean my workbench, which is more like a pile, but I didn't get too far on that one. Some things even unemployment can't fix!

The sense of slowness and waiting even happens when there "is" a job opportunity, but your patience will be tested. You'll hear of an opening and respond quickly because you have time.

If you were looking for a job while employed, it might take you a few days or even a week to respond because your own job and busy schedule wouldn't give you enough time. Now it's time to wait and hear if they're interested. It will seem like forever to you. Unfortunately, this opening isn't the only thing going on for those responsible for the search. All the while you wait, you're wondering what's happening; are they interested or not?

A good friend and I were on the golf course when he asked an interesting question. He said, "Dale, if you knew you'd find a job before you think your money would run out (severance, unused vacation, unemployment, etc.), would you want the job now, or would you prefer to enjoy the time and take it later?" My answer was that I would take it later, relax, and enjoy the time off. He smiled and said, "Then trust and enjoy it."

In this wait, it's a question of trust. In whom do I trust? *I remain confident of this: I will see the goodness of the Lord in the land of the living. Wait for the Lord; be strong and take heart and wait for the Lord* (Psalm 27:13-14).

I trust God, and in this slow time, I wait on him. I know that God is always on time, but rarely early. Place your confidence in God as you wait on him.

TIME IN THE WILDERNESS

WE REALLY DON'T HAVE a wilderness near where I live. Throughout the Bible, God used time in the wilderness to prepare people for his plan and test if they were ready. You are in the wilderness right now, waiting for God to reveal his plan and in this time of waiting, you will be tested.

God allows the devil to tempt us as a test to see how we respond, to see if we are ready for what he has in store for us. Jesus spent time in the desert preparing for his ministry. Most of this account found in Matthew 4:1-11 speaks of Jesus being tempted. *Then Jesus was led by the Spirit into the desert to be tempted by the devil.* (Temptations come when we are tired and worn out, when our resistance is down, and it did for Jesus too.) *After fasting forty days and forty nights, he was hungry. The tempter came to him and ... Jesus said to him, "Away from me, Satan! For it is written: 'Worship the Lord your God and serve him only.'" Then the devil left him, and angels came and attended him.*

There are other stories in the Bible offering accounts of "wilderness" preparation, of being tempted. Read about Joseph (Genesis 37-46) who spent years in one of the worst times in a wilderness under some of the worst difficulties I could ever imagine. He had plenty of opportunities not to trust or to question God, but he didn't. God watched over him until he was ready and said, "It's time" as we find in Genesis 41:41 … *so Pharaoh said to Joseph, "I hereby put you in charge of the whole land of Egypt."* Quite the promotion!

You will get tired and worn out in this process; it's not an easy time. It will be in those days that the devil will come to tempt you. He will whisper thoughts of doubt and what he whispers will be what you fear the most. Although what he whispers to you may be different, some of what he whispered in my ears included:

- "You won't find a job before your severance runs out."
- "You won't find a position as a leader."
- "You might not be able to afford the college where your kids want to go."
- "Your wife might need to go back to work full-time."
- "You won't be able to afford a vacation."

How will you respond? Will you listen to the devil? Will you doubt? Or will you say, "Away with you, devil; I worship the Lord and he's got this." When you call on God's name, he will come and jump in front of the devil and be your shield.

Trust God, not the devil's temptations.

TIME OUT

IF YOU'VE EVER PLAYED, coached, or watched a team sport that has time limits (think football, basketball, hockey, etc.), you know they all have one thing in common: the "time out." Teams take a time out to stop playing, to regroup and adjust.

Usually the team who calls the time out is not doing so well and needs the break to regroup in some manner. It could be to just stop and catch a breath because the pace of the game is too fast, and players are tired. Sometimes it's to figure out a quick way to stop the other team from doing what they're doing well and other times, it might be to figure out what changes need to be made. Time outs may be called by a player who senses things aren't going well, but most often they are called by the coach. Most coaches, but not all, seem to save their time outs for the end of the game when every play and every decision has a major impact on the outcome of the game.

Time outs in life are important too, but the world of work doesn't offer many of them. Unlike other countries in the world, we don't take many breaks. Think about it, though. When you were younger and in school, your life was full of breaks—fall break, Christmas break, spring break, and summer. Each break was a chance to stop, rest up, and get ready for whatever was coming next. One of the harsh realities of being part of the working world is you only get vacation time and vacations tend to be too short. So when life is a little out of sorts, it's hard to regroup.

You are in a "time out" period now, whether you want it or not. This can be a very good thing for any number of reasons. It's possible that things weren't going as well as you would have liked at work, but it wasn't feasible to take time to find a new job. You may need more time with your spouse or your family. You may just need an extended rest.

Often people think God "caused their problems" but he doesn't do that. In Lamentations 3:33 we read, *[God] does not willingly bring affliction or grief to anyone.* But he does "allow" things to happen and then uses them to accomplish his purpose for you. So it just could be that your coach, Jesus Christ, allowed this time out to be called.

Now that you're in the huddle, what is he saying to you? Are you listening or are you talking? James 1:19 reminds us of the order in which we should do things: *My dear brothers and sisters, take note of this: Everyone should be quick to listen, slow to speak and slow to become angry.*

Listen first, that's the key. Please take this "time out" period and be in prayer, listening for what God wants for you in your life.

I'M TIRED; I NEED SOME ENERGY

THE JOURNEY YOU FIND yourself on is more marathon than a sprint. Sprinters have a big burst of energy, run a short distance as fast as they can, and the race is over quickly. Marathon runners go a long distance and need to conserve energy and be consistent in their use of it. But on such a long journey, it's easy to "hit a wall" and run out of energy.

The same is true for your marathon. You get tired and want to give up. Don't think you're the only one who has done that; some quit. They say forget it, I don't want to do this anymore, I'm done. I'll just work part-time somewhere to make a little money.

You may be there right now. You've spent months doing the same things, searching for the next opportunity. You're networking with anyone you can, following up on every opening you hear about, searching online, etc., etc. But with no results. You're just tired and want to quit.

Don't quit.

Isaiah 40:28-31 can help with this challenge. *Do you not know? Have you not heard? The Lord is the everlasting God, the Creator of the ends of the earth. He will not grow tired or weary, and his understanding no one can fathom.* ***He gives strength to the weary and increases the power of the weak.*** *Even youths grow tired and weary, and young men stumble and fall;* ***but those who hope in the Lord will renew their strength.*** *They will soar on wings like eagles; they will run and not grow weary, they will walk and not be faint.*

On this journey, it isn't a question of if we'll get tired, it's a question of when. Lucky for us God never gets tired. Look back over the verses from Isaiah. When you or I tire, he gives us strength to carry on. And as our strength is renewed, so is our hope.

We often miss the many ways God renews our strength. We don't even realize how he uses his power to energize us. It could come from taking a day off from your job search or getting away for a weekend with your spouse, or listening to an inspirational speaker who energizes you, or in helping someone else who needs you. In whatever way that burst of energy comes, recognize that was God, it's his unexpected and amazing grace.

Keep your hope and trust in him. He'll make sure you have energy in your batteries to keep going.

NOT IF, BUT WHEN

I'M AT BREAKFAST FOR a networking meeting at another Panera Bread. I think I've been in at least one or more each week on this journey. They're always full and when I look around, I'm not the only person having a networking meeting. Today breakfast is with Rick, whom I didn't know until our meeting. What a wonderful man of God, who had also gone through this journey.

What I liked most about Rick was what he was doing now—not his job, but his passion for helping others (like me) in networking and finding a new job. Rick was the essence of what's described in 1 Thessalonians 5:11—*Therefore encourage one another and build each other up, just as in fact you are doing.* Rick was an encourager, one of many I've met on my journey. I pray I will be as good as him in encouraging others.

Our conversation covered a variety of topics, but at least twice he reminded me that it's not *if* I'll ever find a new job, it's *when* I'll find a new job. While this is a simple concept, it's an important one. When we are on this journey and nothing is happening, it's easy to begin to think that it never will happen. But that's a lie the devil keeps whispering into our ears. Don't believe the lie.

The unknown always throws us off; the unknown scares us

and we don't know how to deal with it. The challenge you and I face is waiting and not knowing "when" it will happen. If you could look into the future and see that in six months you'd be starting a new job, you would probably say "Okay, I can wait six months. It might not be easy, but in the big picture, it's a small amount of time." Once you knew that, you'd probably relax and start to enjoy the extra time you have available. That's why Rick was reminding me, it will happen, so relax.

Right now, we're going through a trial of sorts, a tough time. We need to remember that this trial is only **temporary**. As we read in 1 Peter 1:6-7, *In all this you greatly rejoice, though now for a little while you may have had to suffer grief in all kinds of trials. These have come so that the proven genuineness of your faith—of greater worth than gold, which perishes even though refined by fire— may result in praise, glory and honor when Jesus Christ is revealed.*

I have no doubt that my faith is being tested on this journey. Yours is being tested too. But when the waiting ends, and we look back, we'll agree that it was well worth the wait.

FEELING FORGOTTEN

I'M FEELING FORGOTTEN THESE days. I'm feeling alone. I spend much more time by myself. At times I reflect and think about the people I worked with. I wonder how they are doing and how they are dealing with issues without me. I wonder if they ever think of me. I don't feel very needed. How about you?

If you get a moment, go take a rock of any size. Walk to a small pond or lake and throw it in the water. Watch what you see happening. First, there will be a splash in the water and the bigger the rock, the bigger the splash. Regardless of the size of the rock, it will quickly go out of sight under water. Then you'll see some ripples going out from the splash and soon the water will look just like it did before you threw the rock into it.

I feel like that rock.

I was in the same place for 25 years. I knew many people and many knew me. I felt like I was a big rock. What I realize now is that life quickly returned to normal for those I left behind. Me? I'm feeling alone and forgotten. How about you right now?

It's not uncommon to lose touch with those with whom you worked for a variety of reasons. It's certainly not intentional on anyone's part. When you left your job, there was more work for those left behind, so they are very busy. You've also lost one of the things you had in common—your work. Conversations are much easier when we have something in common. Another reason might be that your friends are uncomfortable at the thought of talking to you. What do they say? Remember, they are sorry for you, and they may also be glad it wasn't them.

Even though I might feel alone, I know that I'm not. I can't see it, but God's connected to me, holding my hand and yours, too. *Yet I am always with you; you hold me by my right hand* (Psalm 73:23).

When he holds our hand, it's to remind us we aren't alone, he's there with us. And because he's with us, we shouldn't be afraid. *For I am the Lord your God who takes hold of your right hand and says to you, "Do not fear; I will help you"* (Isaiah 41:13).

When you're sitting alone, feeling forgotten, picture yourself walking alongside your heavenly father; he's holding your hand and you don't have a care in the world. What a great visual to keep in mind.

WHAT ARE YOU DOING WITH YOUR BODY?

IT WAS CHRISTMAS 2002 when my wife gave me an unexpected gift. She had been exercising regularly at a fitness club near where she worked and gave me a free month trial at the same club. For years I stayed in shape by playing basketball during the winter, but I wasn't playing much basketball anymore. I tried the fitness center and it was different for me. New equipment, a new regimen for me, and it was different doing it all on my own. Basketball is a team sport and I enjoyed the camaraderie and the exercise. At the end of January, I told my wife I didn't think I wanted to continue, it wasn't for me.

A week later, on February 5, my boss told me he was eliminating my job. My life began to change drastically. The next week to ten days were difficult having to say good-bye to people I'd worked with for years and walking into the unknown of not having a job after 25 years. To say it was stressful would be a bit of an understatement. I knew I needed to do something with my time, so I told my wife I wanted to join her fitness club. I began a regular workout schedule and today, 15 years later, I continue to work out. It's become an important discipline for me.

Does Scripture refer to working out? No. But there are references to our health. One such reference is 1 Corinthians 6:19-20. *Do you not know that your bodies are temples of the Holy Spirit, who is in you, whom you have received from God? You are not your own; you were bought at a price. Therefore, honor God with your bodies.* God wants us to take care of the body he gave us.

My question for you is this: What are you doing with your body? Are you taking care of yourself these days? For many, exercise is an afterthought—it comes after doing everything else on the to-do list. It's not a priority. But maybe it should be a priority. You have more time on your hands than you've had in a long time, which is a great opportunity; but it can also be a challenge. The challenge is you're around the house more and there are probably all sorts of snacks available to eat. I'm not against snacks; I enjoy them myself, but in moderation. You might convince yourself you "need a break," which means more time on the couch watching TV or surfing online. Are you watching what you eat?

Please take this opportunity to do something for yourself. If you've been exercising, keep it up and maybe do it more often. If you haven't been exercising lately, take this chance to start. It can be as simple as walking, getting out in your neighborhood multiple times in a week. Walking is good for your health and for me, a 30-minute walk on the track is a 30-minute conversation with God. If you can afford it, join a gym and begin a regular workout.

Exercise helps your body and reduces stress. Please take care of yourself during this break from work. You'll be glad you did.

DAYS OF DESPAIR

WE'VE ALREADY TALKED ABOUT the days when you feel mad or angry, the days you want to scream and cry out. What we haven't talked about is despair, that feeling of hopelessness that comes crashing down upon you. You just might experience despair from time to time. It will come in those days when nothing is happening, and you begin to think: there is no job for me, this will never end, I'm never going to get out of this. And on days of despair, our hope disappears.

Despair isn't unique to you or what you are experiencing. Even the Apostle Paul felt despair as we read of his pain in 2 Corinthians 1:8-10. *We do not want you to be uninformed, brothers and sisters, about the troubles we experienced in the province of Asia. We were under great pressure, far beyond our ability to endure, so that we despaired of life itself. Indeed, we felt we had received the sentence of death. But this happened that we might not rely on ourselves but on God, who raises the dead. He has delivered us from such a deadly peril, and he will deliver us again. On him we have set our hope that he will continue to deliver us.*

Do you feel as if you have more than you can endure? The good news for us is that even in days of despair, we have a Savior who came to wipe out the despair, the tears, and the hopelessness.

He can use our despair to draw us closer to him, to give us hope again. Listening is one of the best, if not the best way, to show you care. If one of your children or friends is having a bad day, what do you do for them? You take time out to sit and to listen. God loves us even more. He wants us to reach out to him and he will listen. The Apostle Peter is specific about this when he says, *Cast all your anxiety on him because he cares for you* (1 Peter 5:7).

Give God all your frustration, bitterness, feelings of being lost or hopeless or alone. He can take it and he'll help carry your burden. In Matthew 11:28-30, Jesus said, *Come to me, all you who are weary and burdened, and I will give you rest. Take my yoke upon you and learn from me, for I am gentle and humble in heart, and you will find rest for your souls. For my yoke is easy and my burden is light.* A yoke is designed to divide the load, to share it. So here Jesus is saying, "Give me your problems and they'll be my problems. I'll lend a hand to help you and the burden won't be so heavy." He also says, "I'm there for you and I'll always be there for you, because I love you."

He gives us back hope. Give a good shout of anguish to God today. Maybe cry. Tears are a good way to release your pain. Then let God share your burden and divide your despair.

HALFTIME

IT'S DECEMBER 23 AS I write this; time for the traditional "Bragging Rights" basketball game between the University of Missouri and the University of Illinois. It's college basketball at its best. I didn't go to either school, but loving college basketball and growing up in St. Louis, it's just a game you have to watch. Before they even have a sweat up, Missouri is behind, and it keeps getting worse. Time outs are called to make those quick adjustments to break the momentum. Halftime in a game is when adjustments are made, minor and/or major based on how the game is going.

This time in your life might be your "halftime," time to think about and consider adjustments. You've probably had many successes in your career so far, but this period of unemployment most likely wasn't part of your planning. Instead of just picking up and moving on to do the same thing you've been doing with a different company, you have some time available to pause and reflect. Ask yourself some important questions about your life, your work, and where you are going. A good friend of mine told me about a book called *Halftime* by Bob Buford that I purchased early in my unemployment and read. It's excellent, and I encourage you to read it too. It will help you look at where you are, what you are good at, and what you want to do with the rest of your working life. What will your priorities be?

Asking these questions doesn't necessarily mean you need to change your career; then again, this might be the time. This might be a time God has given you to reevaluate your priorities and to steer you in a different direction. Or he might use this time to reenergize you. My prayer is that you are open to considering that God might be ready to use the special gifts he's given you in ways different than you had previously imagined.

Throughout the Bible, we find people who were quite content in what they were doing until God said, "I have other plans for you." Moses learned that in Exodus 3:9-10. *And now the cry of the Israelites has reached me, and I have seen the way the Egyptians are oppressing them. So now, go. I am sending you to Pharaoh to bring my people the Israelites out of Egypt.* The Apostle Peter thought he'd spend his life as a fisherman until in Matthew 4:18-20 Jesus told him to stop his fishing and come with him. *As Jesus was walking beside the Sea of Galilee, he saw two brothers, Simon called Peter and his brother Andrew. They were casting a net into the lake, for they were fishermen. "Come, follow me," Jesus said, "and I will send you out to fish for people." At once they left their nets and followed him.*

My encouragement for you is to stay in dialog with God and use this time to think about the future and what's next for you.

I'M AT THE BOTTOM OF THE PIT; I WANT TO GIVE UP

THE FEELING OF HOPELESSNESS is upon me. I've been searching for a new job, but I haven't found one. I feel like I'm looking for a "needle in a haystack." I'm overqualified for most of the jobs I hear or learn about and even if they would take me, I know the job isn't for me. Do I want to have just "a job"? Absolutely not! I want something that's right for me, where my gifts will be needed.

The time is dragging on and I try to stay positive, but I'm very tired of it all. When I see people, I'm tired of saying all those positive "clichés" I know I should say, "I know God has plans for me," "When the door closed, I know another will soon be opening," and on, and on, and on. I'm tired of this. I want to quit! It feels hopeless.

Many of the psalms are expressions of hopelessness. King David must have felt as I do right now. You can read all of Psalm 69, but these are the verses I read repeatedly when I feel like this. *Save me, O God, for the waters have come up to my neck. I sink in the miry depths, where there is no foothold. I have come into the deep waters; the floods engulf me. I am worn out calling for help; my throat is parched. My eyes fail, looking for my God.*

Do you feel this way right now, the waters up around your neck, no place to put your feet? You've been calling for help, but no answers come? Read on.

But I pray to you, O Lord, in the time of your favor; in your great love, O God, answer me with your sure salvation. Rescue me from the mire, do not let me sink; deliver me from those who hate me, from the deep waters. Do not let the floodwaters engulf me or the depths swallow me up or the pit close its mouth over me. Answer me, O Lord, out of the goodness of your love; in your great mercy turn to me. Do not hide your face from your servant; answer me quickly, for I am in trouble. Come near and rescue me; redeem me because of my foes.

You might not see them, but I'm shedding tears, at least on the inside, because I hurt. I want to just quit! I must be patient for God to provide the right opportunity. If I quit, I'm giving up on God and saying I don't have faith that he will come through. I love and enjoy playing golf. In the great golfer Jack Nicklaus' autobiography, he talked about winning tournaments—even when he wasn't playing his best—just by not quitting and staying in the game. When he didn't quit, he had a chance to regain his rhythm and play better. Then he regained his confidence and the next thing he knew, he had won. You too can win, if you don't quit.

Continue as I do to trust in God. He will deliver me, and he will deliver you.

WHY DOESN'T HIS GRACE SEEM SUFFICIENT ENOUGH?

I HAVE IT ALL. I'm a baptized child of God, assured that I will spend all of eternity in heaven with my Savior. I don't doubt it for a minute. I know that he died for my sins and in his death and resurrection, I became saved. I should be jumping up and down with joy these days, but I'm not.

Why? These days, my life has been turned upside down and I can't get it fixed. Did you notice those words I used, "I can't"? That's a problem for me and maybe it's a problem for you. Too much of me trying to do it all. I'm unemployed for the first time in my life. I'm wondering where I'll be working next. I'm wondering why this happened? What will everyone be thinking about me? I'm questioning everything.

But it's not about me doing, it's about me receiving from God. *My grace is sufficient for you, for my power is made perfect in weakness* (2 Corinthians 12:9).

I'm working hard to find the right job for me. I'm good at doing things. I'm sending out resumes, calling people I know, networking, and doing all the things you're supposed to do. But nothing has happened. I'm good at what I do, I really am, so there should be someone who wants me. But there isn't, at least not yet. I don't know why.

But it's not about me doing, it's about me receiving from God. *My grace is sufficient for you, for my power is made perfect in weakness* (2 Corinthians 12:9).

I know that I can't get this done on my own. I know the answer is to turn my pain and concerns over to God, but I just can't seem to let go. I want to give him my burden, but I can't seem to give it up. I'm holding on too tight. It's hard to let someone else take over and not worry about it.

But it's not about me doing, it's about me receiving from God. *But he said to me, "My grace is sufficient for you, for my power is made perfect in weakness"* (2 Corinthians 12:9).

God wants us to admit that we cannot do this on our own and rest in his awesome power. If you've been hanging on as much as I tend to, please let go and let God take over. My new job will be an unbelievable gift from God.

UNWELCOME NEWS

YOU'LL HAVE DAYS WHEN you receive "unwelcome" news related to your job search. I received unwelcome news today when I learned a position I had applied for and was very interested in was "pretty far along in their process." Those were words I read from someone who works there, although I have not yet been contacted. Which most likely, but not always, means I won't have a chance to interview and they'll choose someone else. Unwelcome news can change your mood instantly from feeling pretty good and happy to sad and anxious. I went from feeling great to taking a nosedive just by reading an email. It will happen to you too, and your family and friends won't even realize why.

Why are we impacted this way? Most of us apply for jobs that seem to be a good match for us with an organization we like or respect. When we apply, we invest some of what I call "emotional capital" in the process—e.g., we try to picture ourselves at the organization, doing the job we've applied for. We begin to imagine things we might do there and what it feels like to be employed once again. Those are confidence builders. But when we get news that it probably won't happen, anxiety creeps in as we cross another opportunity off our list of possibilities. One might even begin to worry and ask, "Will I ever find a job?"

When this happens, it's time to redirect our thoughts. In Jeremiah 29:11, God spoke these words through the prophet: *"For I know the plans I have for you," declares the Lord, "plans to prosper you and not to harm you, plans to give you hope and a future."* God's plan is for you to prosper, to be successful, to flourish. He doesn't want you in a place that won't be good for you. You may have thought it was a great job opportunity, but then you realize that perhaps it wasn't. If that job was not a place where you would prosper, then God doesn't want it for you. But also know that if that particular job is part of God's plan for you and for some reason the search had been thwarted, that they will come back to you, because our God is stronger than those conducting their search.

Fear and anxiety are bound to creep back into your world. When it does, turn to God and put your trust in him. *When I am afraid, I put my trust in you. In God, whose word I praise—in God I trust and am not afraid. What can mere mortals do to me?* (Psalm 56:3-4).

One more thing—resist the desire to lie around and feel sorry for yourself. Keep moving, pressing on toward the goal of finding the job that God has in store for you.

WHEN COUNTING WORKS AGAINST YOU

IT'S NATURAL TO WANT to know how you are doing, whether it's in golf or bowling or work. You're able to compare your performance against someone else's or against a standard. In business, we use metrics to compare performance against an expected standard. But such a comparison along your journey of unemployment won't help; it's not a good thing to do.

I did it by counting and maybe you do it too. I counted anniversary dates—February 5, February 14, September 11, October 11. February 5 is when I was told my job was being eliminated and on February 14 I walked out of the hospital where I had worked for almost 25 years. September 11 and October 11 are the dates corresponding to my last employer. Ask someone who is unemployed, and I'll wager they know their "anniversary" date or dates.

Such dates can also trigger some counting—one month gone (unemployed), two months gone, etc. Or you might count in reverse; for example, if you have severance and savings you estimate will cover you four months, you might count three months left, two months left, etc.

This is not a healthy use of numbers. You can't manage this journey like you would work; comparisons can only frustrate you and bring on anxiety. Counting may happen unintentionally, but it will happen. When it does, you might feel like what the Apostle Paul describes in Romans 7:15-20. *I do not understand what I do. For what I want to do I do not do, but what I hate I do. And if I do what I do not want to do, I agree that the law is good. As it is, it is no longer I myself who do it, but it is sin living in me. For I know that good itself does not dwell in me, that is, in my sinful nature. For I have the desire to do what is good, but I cannot carry it out. For I do not do the good I want to do, but the evil I do not want to do—this I keep on doing. Now if I do what I do not want to do, it is no longer I who do it, but it is sin living in me that does it.*

That's me … I don't know why I do it, but I do it and I hate myself for doing it. I'm ashamed at how many times I've let counting in some manner affect my trust in God. We forget that God's math doesn't match anything in this world and he doesn't care about the numbers. He only cares about us.

Thankfully he loves us so much that he forgives our lack of trust. He's sitting right by us saying, "Stop looking at numbers; rely on me. I've got this. I love you!"

Now that's something we can count on!

WAITING IS HARD

MOST OF US AREN'T very good at waiting. I'm certainly not. Our lives tend to be a rush—rushing here and there. We're very proud we can "multitask," doing more than one thing at a time. We want everything instantly, and therein lies one of the biggest challenges as you search, because things won't happen instantly.

The waiting in the job search process will test you because you'll do lots and lots of waiting. The good news with this waiting though, is that God wants to use it for doing good things for us. *Yet the Lord longs to be gracious to you; therefore he will rise up to show you compassion. For the Lord is a God of justice. Blessed are all who wait for him* (Isaiah 30:18).

Think about it: Some things take time to turn out good. In cooking, that's especially true. I love fudge, which we make at Christmas each year. To make exceptional fudge, you need to bring the ingredients to a rolling boil very slowly. It usually takes me a half hour to do it right and if I don't, the sugar won't dissolve properly, which makes grainy fudge. If you like good risotto, you can't make it in ten minutes; it'll take you close to a half-hour.

How about children? I have three awesome sons and four grandchildren. None of them came quickly; they all came at about nine months as planned. Two of my sons were even late by a couple of weeks. I have three beautiful daughters-in-law, but I had to wait for them too—waiting for their relationship with my sons to develop, to agree to be married, and to plan a wedding. Was all the waiting worth it for our family? Absolutely!

The job search process is full of waiting and the speed it moves isn't dictated by you. You'll need to *wait* for there to be a job opening that matches your gifts, *wait* for the organization to review your application and decide to interview you, *wait* for the day of the interview, *wait* for a second interview, as most organizations want to see you twice and have you meet different people in the process, *wait* for an offer. And if there is no offer, the process starts over somewhere else. A "no" simply means it wasn't part of God's plan for you, and even though you must continue to *wait* and it will take longer than you'd like, you can't control making it happen more quickly.

What do we do during this waiting process? We trust in God and have faith that he will provide the right opportunity.

WHERE EVERYBODY KNOWS YOUR NAME

REMEMBER THE TV SHOW *Cheers* from the early 1990s? It was centered around people who worked at, or regularly visited, a bar. The theme song was "Where everybody knows your name." It was a "community" of people who enjoyed being with each other, who teased each other, who laughed and cried together.

Work provided "community" for us. You may not have loved everyone you worked with, but you enjoyed most of them. Most of us spend more hours with the people we work with than we do with our family. I had a team that I worked with and I had a team who reported to me. I knew many of their family members and, at the very least, heard stories about their families.

I miss them. It makes me sad that I don't see them regularly. I miss the chance to affirm them and be affirmed by them. While I may stay connected and remain friends with those I enjoyed the most, I may never work with any of them again. It's left a hole in my life that I haven't yet replaced.

How about you? Do you have that hole in your life right now?

There is a tendency for many in our situation to withdraw, to not be around others. That's the exact opposite of what we need to do. Community has always been very important. God did not create us to be alone, especially at a time like this. Community is where we can glean support and encouragement. Hebrews 10:24-25 reminds us that in community we "spur one another on" and not to give up "meeting together." *And let us consider how we may spur one another on toward love and good deeds, not giving up meeting together, as some are in the habit of doing, but encouraging one another—and all the more as you see the Day approaching.*

Spend time with good friends and family. Reconnect with those you haven't spent much time with because you were previously "busy working." People will welcome a chance to be with you because they are part of your community and they hurt for you. Focus on 1 Corinthians 12:26, especially as it talks about how the body all works together. *If one part suffers, every part suffers with it; if one part is honored, every part rejoices with it.*

Don't miss the opportunity to expand your community, especially with those who are in a similar situation. If you know someone else who is out of work, reach out and get together. You can be community for each other.

HOW'S YOUR SEARCH GOING?

HOW'S YOUR SEARCH GOING? I get that question quite often. Others want to ask the question but hold back because they're not sure what the answer is or how the question will affect me.

My answer is pretty much the same whenever I'm asked, but how it impacts me emotionally is different depending on what's going on. Most days, my reaction and emotions are good. The question tells me they care and are interested enough to ask. That's a good thing and I'm happy to answer. Some days though, I'll admit to groaning internally as I say to myself, *"Ugghhh, do I really have to answer this again? There hasn't been any change. The answer is the same as it was the last time. I need to be positive about this, but I don't really feel like being positive."* Has that ever happened to you? I'll bet it has and that's okay. It's a normal feeling.

How do you answer the question? I believe that each time we're asked becomes an important opportunity. Others are watching to see how we react. In this simple little question, we have a chance to give witness to what we believe and in whom we trust. It's a chance to demonstrate our faith to others.

Is our faith the same as the faith described in Romans 4:18-21? *Against all hope, Abraham in hope believed and so became the father of many nations, just as it had been said to him, "So shall your offspring be." Without weakening in his faith, he faced the fact that his body was as good as dead—since he was about a hundred years old—and that Sarah's womb was also dead. Yet he did not waver through unbelief regarding the promise of God but was strengthened in his faith and gave glory to God, being fully persuaded that God had power to do what he had promised.* It's tough to have hope when nothing is happening, but our challenge isn't nearly as difficult as Abraham's. What I love in this text is when it says he didn't waver; he was strengthened and gave glory to God. Every time we answer the question posed to us, we can give the glory to God. And I believe that in doing so, we will be strengthened.

So here's what my answer looks like: "So far, there hasn't been the right opportunity available for me. I knew this was going to take some time, so I'm learning to be patient. But I know God has something amazing in store for me. I'm trusting him and know he'll reveal it to me in his time." It's not a perfect answer, but I can tell you with all honesty that my faith got stronger each time I said the words.

My answer reminds people that it's God where I put my faith and my trust. Every time I say it, I get more content in my waiting for his plans to be revealed. It's going to be a great day when that offer comes. I can't wait.

MAYBE YOU HAVEN'T OPENED THE RIGHT DOOR

WHEN I FIRST BECAME unemployed, many who saw me passed on words of encouragement. Two of the most common were that "God has other plans for you" and "When one door closes, another door will be opened." I liked both because they implied there would be a new job for me at a new place and, in my mind, it was just around the corner.

In Matthew 7:7-12, Jesus talks about "asking." *Ask and it will be given to you; seek and you will find; knock and the door will be opened to you. For everyone who asks receives; the one who seeks finds; and to the one who knocks, the door will be opened. Which of you, if your son asks for bread, will give him a stone? Or if he asks for a fish, will give him a snake? If you, then, though you are evil, know how to give good gifts to your children, how much more will your Father in heaven give good gifts to those who ask him! So in everything, do to others what you would have them do to you, for this sums up the Law and the Prophets.* So I prayed and prayed and prayed. I was in regular dialog with God, but nothing happened. Days turned into weeks and the weeks turned into months and then more months, with nothing opening for me.

I was often encouraged to go into the consulting field; I'd thank them for their kind words but said I'm not much of an entrepreneur. At my 25th wedding anniversary, a friend strongly encouraged me to consider providing human resources support for small businesses. I pushed it off as maybe someone who had too much to drink that evening. Shortly after that, another friend said almost the same thing and I began to think about it. Soon the idea was never very far from my mind and I began to talk about it with friends whose opinions I trusted.

When talking about it with a very dear friend, she said that maybe nothing had opened for me because going into business for myself was the door God wanted me to open. It hit me out the blue: God doesn't say which door will be opened to us. In my time off, I had directed my time toward one door, the one I was familiar with and felt most comfortable with. How about you? If nothing is happening in your search, maybe it's time to ask if there are other doors for you to consider, maybe even a door you've been avoiding?

At the end of his book *That's a Winner!* baseball Hall of Fame broadcaster Jack Buck thanked all the people who ever fired him because it gave him a new opportunity to do something he probably wouldn't have done on his own. Jack was right. You now have an opportunity that may not have come had this not happened. It doesn't make the days go by more quickly or maybe make you feel better, but God gives us what we need, and he won't let us down.

With God as your guide, you will be successful in whatever door he opens for you. Just start looking at all the possibilities.

GOD PROVIDES

I ENJOYED A "CUP of coffee"—okay, it was really a Diet Coke—with Terry today. Terry's employer combined regions and as a result, Terry needed to reapply for his job. He didn't get the new job. That put him, like me and like you, in a time of waiting on God. What's next?

As we talked, Terry told me he's had more time to read Scripture and, in his reading, he read the book of Jonah. Terry remarked that he noticed the phrase "God provided" four times in the book of Jonah. It's an interesting phrase because the writer of Jonah is looking back in time at what happened, so God's "providing" was in the past. We both talked about how hard it can be to see all that God is doing and providing when we're in the middle of a difficult time. You might feel that way right now. You might even find yourself asking, what did God do for me other than allow me to be unemployed?

It's always easier to look back and see all that God has done for us. It's in looking back that we see how we were shaped or prepared for what was to come. We're able to see how his plan came together for us. In the future, I think you'll probably be able to look back and see what a blessing this period of unemployment was and how God provided for you. Over the years, I've worked with a few individuals who lost their jobs at a time their parent or spouse was ill and dying. Their job loss allowed them to focus 100% on the person they loved and not feel guilty about it.

What we want is often different than what we need—I may want a lot of things, but I don't need them all. What does God tell us about our needs? *And my God will meet all your needs according to the riches of his glory in Christ Jesus* (Philippians 4:19). *His divine power has given us everything we need for a godly life through our knowledge of him who called us by his own glory and goodness* (2 Peter 1:3). In these two Scripture verses we learn that he'll meet "all" of our needs and that he's give us "everything" we need.

When I look back, I realize he provided me severance pay and unemployment compensation as income sources, he provided people for me to network with who usually picked up the bill for the meal we ate, he provided friends to listen to me, my vehicles had no major repairs and were in no accidents, my overall health was good (other than a cold or the flu), and there were no major home repairs. I could go on and on with what he has done for me. He's doing the same for you.

Take a moment to pause and look for the many ways he has provided for you, your daily needs and some of those unnecessary, but greatly appreciated, gifts of his grace. Rejoice in all he provides!

THE RELIEF PITCHER

A NEW FRIEND I met in my networking, Benjamin, suggested that being in transition between jobs is like being a "relief pitcher" in baseball. If you don't know much about relief pitchers, let me tell you about them. Relief pitchers don't start the game, they sit away from the rest of the team out in the "bullpen" waiting for a call to come into the game. Usually, they get called into the game when there is a need—or even a crisis of some sort—and are asked to solve it, usually by getting the other team out without any runs scoring. They come into the game well rested and full of energy. Some games, they never get called. In fact, for relief pitchers, it could be many games before they are needed, but they need to be prepared for that call.

He was right; if you're out of work looking for a new job, you are a "relief pitcher." You're waiting for the call and the challenge you face is that you don't know *when*, which is the hardest part. So you wait, and wait, and wait. The waiting is hard and gets harder the longer you must wait. As you read this, I imagine you've been looking for a job for some time, but you haven't found one yet. Your life has a different rhythm and you might even be comfortable with that rhythm. But if you get too comfortable, you might not be prepared when the call comes.

In Matthew 24, we are reminded to always be ready, because we know God is coming. *Therefore keep watch, because you do not know on what day your Lord will come. But understand this: If the owner of the house had known at what time of night the thief was coming, he would have kept watch and would not have let his house be broken into. So you also must be ready, because the Son of Man will come at an hour when you do not expect him* (Matthew 24:42-44). While being ready for a new job isn't the same as Christ returning, it's wise to be ready. A good relief pitcher is ready all the time. Are you ready?

What if someone called today and wanted to interview you over the phone, would you be ready to make a positive impression? If your answer is "yes," good for you. If not, take the time to prepare for an interview. (See Appendix E for some assistance.) What else might you do to prepare for a return to work?

Have you been working at improving your job skills or adding new ones while looking for a job? This is a great opportunity to do so, especially for something like technology. We can all use better technology skills and it changes so quickly. What about your mind? Are you actively reading and learning new things that will help you when you are back "in the game"? If not, get started.

A challenge you face in this process is that there is very little you can control. You don't control what jobs become open, when they come open or if the hiring manager is interested in you. What you can control is your own preparation. Do what you can do, prepare yourself and be ready for the call and a chance to get back into the game. It will come.

DISCERNMENT: IS THIS THE RIGHT ONE FOR ME?

CHOICES AND DECISIONS. I don't know about you, but I work hard at making the best decision possible. I'm analytical in my approach to decision making, trying to look at all angles. I'll admit sometimes I try to make the "perfect" decision and then second-guess myself. I expect you might even get interviews with a couple of different organizations at the same time. Life usually clumps up on us and we go from nothing to almost too much. How do we make the right choice and look for the right things?

When I think about choosing, I am reminded of when David was anointed to be king over Israel, which is detailed in 1 Samuel 16. God told Samuel to anoint the next king; he was to go see Jesse of Bethlehem and God would tell him which of Jesse's sons was the right one. He arrived and Jesse brought out his sons. Read what happened: *When they arrived, Samuel saw Eliab and thought, "Surely the Lord's anointed stands here before the Lord." But the Lord said to Samuel, "Do not consider his appearance or his height, for I have rejected him. The Lord does not look at the things people look at. People look at the outward appearance, but the*

Lord looks at the heart." Then Jesse called Abinadab and had him pass in front of Samuel. But Samuel said, "The Lord has not chosen this one either." Jesse then had Shammah pass by, but Samuel said, "Nor has the Lord chosen this one." Jesse had seven of his sons pass before Samuel, but Samuel said to him, "The Lord has not chosen these." So he asked Jesse, "Are these all the sons you have?" "There is still the youngest," Jesse answered. "He is tending the sheep." Samuel said, "Send for him; we will not sit down until he arrives." So he sent for him and had him brought in. He was glowing with health and had a fine appearance and handsome features. Then the Lord said, "Rise and anoint him; this is the one." So Samuel took the horn of oil and anointed him in the presence of his brothers, and from that day on the Spirit of the Lord came powerfully upon David. Samuel then went to Ramah (1 Samuel 16:6-13).

Jesse kept parading his son's in front of Samuel asking, "What about this one?" "Okay, not him, what about him?" and on and on. They all looked good, how you'd expect a king to look. But God looked past outward appearances in making his decision; he looked at the "heart." I encourage you to do the same.

Your decision shouldn't be about who will pay you the most money, or who has the best 401(k), or bonus, etc. Your decision should be based upon what is the best match for the gifts and abilities God has given you. That's what he wants for you—a place where you'll find joy, where you will thrive and flourish.

Pray to God for guidance and look for the "heart" of the job as you decide.

HE GRANTS THE DESIRES OF OUR HEARTS

TAKE TIME TO READ Psalm 37. What a great psalm it is! Take special note of verse 4: *Delight yourself in the Lord and he will give you the desires of your heart!* This is a favorite phrase of my wife's and she has used it for years. Sometimes I don't think I really believed it, but after what I've been through, I know it is true. How easy it is to forget that God knows us better than we know ourselves. He knows what is deep down inside of us—our desires, our hopes, and our fears. Most of these we don't express to even our closest friends or family.

I have experienced more emotional pain on this journey than I have in a long time. During this painful process, God granted some special desires that he knew were in my heart. Your deep desires will be different than mine, I'm sure. I've always wanted to be more at peace, a peace that accepts God being in control, not me. I struggled to break away from "doing it on my own." I'm a "Type A" personality, one who is constantly driving to achieve and be successful. And try as I might, I couldn't achieve that peace. Yet through the experience, I was granted a peace I had never experienced before. For some reason, I wasn't worried about what was going to happen. You can say it was because I had a decent severance pay package, but money doesn't solve our problems and I knew it wouldn't bring me peace. I had prayed for God to release me from my struggle and in taking my job away, I was released.

I also wanted to be closer to my wife, children, and friends. I knew I needed more time with them but could never seem to fit it into the schedule. Boy did God ever give me time! The question was would I use it the right way. Finally, I had some personal activities I wanted to enjoy, golf being toward the top. With time available, my wife and I were able to visit one of my oldest friends and mentors on Hilton Head Island to watch the PGA tour's Heritage Classic. Later in the fall, I took a temporary project working in the Pocono Mountains. The tough part was being away from my family; the good part was doing things I would not normally get a chance to do. I slept in the car to get an early tee time to play the Black Course at Bethpage State Park (it's a tradition to do this), the site of the 2002 and 2009 US Opens. I broke 80 for the first time at Shawnee on the Delaware, home of the 1938 PGA Championship. Finally, my family visited at Thanksgiving and we all saw the Macy's Thanksgiving Day parade.

Our Heavenly Father knows us better than we know ourselves. We forget that God is a father first, and don't fathers want the best for their children? You just might be surprised to discover the many ways he grants exactly what we need.

HELPING HANDS AND WORDS OF ENCOURAGEMENT

WHEN I FOUND OUT my job was eliminated, I was hurt and felt very alone, even though there were others from my organization impacted just like me. In my mind, of course, the biggest effect was on me. In my feelings of being alone, I was blessed to be showered by phone calls and cards. Some even came with M&Ms (my favorite candy), so much so, that I walked out of my office on my last day with more than 40 pounds of M&Ms. Some calls came from people I hadn't worked with in more than ten years.

I learned that friendships went deeper than I imagined and found that many had been in my shoes at some time. Cards came from people I never imagined would care enough to send a note. I even received a visit from a high school classmate who had heard the news and just had to come by to see me. It was a wonderfully affirming time. My friends were encouraging me at a time when I really needed it. I guess they must have all read 1 Thessalonians 5:11, where it says *Therefore encourage one another and build each other up, just as in fact you are doing.*

As I look back, I realize I've known many people who lost

their jobs. Some I took the time to send a note to or call, but many I didn't. I'm embarrassed to say that I was just "too busy." I can't undo the past, but the question I ask myself is what will I do in the future? Having been in those shoes and knowing what it feels like gives us an opportunity to help others in a way we'd never have imagined.

I believe you and I have a responsibility to help others. In 2 Corinthians 1:3-4 we are told that God comforts us so that we can comfort others. *Praise be to the God and Father of our Lord Jesus Christ, the Father of compassion and the God of all comfort, who comforts us in all our troubles, so that we can comfort those in any trouble with the comfort we ourselves have received from God.*

There's something very special about a call or visit from someone who "really" understands what you are going through, who has "walked in your shoes." You now will have a special bond with others who lose their job and you reaching out to them will mean a great deal. Whether or not you know them well, take the time to send a personal note of encouragement, to call, or stop by.

Yes, it takes time—something you may have too much of today but may not when you're back to work. But remember what it meant to you and realize that what you have to offer will mean so much to them.

HE RESTORES MY SOUL

THE 23RD PSALM IS a beautiful psalm. I memorized it as a child. As sometimes happens, they were words that didn't have much meaning to me. I could answer questions about what they meant (I listened to the teacher) but when I really faced adversity, the words began to really mean something.

Unemployment for me was real adversity. When I lost my job, I lost a part of me. Even though I didn't get fired, I lost some of my self-confidence. I felt like I had "lost my soul"; I lost being me. I had seen it before in others. You can see it in their eyes when they're between jobs; they too, had lost something. Now it had happened to me. When people ask how we're doing, we probably give the standard answers, things like "I'm fine," "I know I'll find something soon," etc. After all, we can't say what we probably feel: "I'm doing terrible," "I don't think I can be successful ever again," etc. People would run away.

Let's look at the first two verses of Psalm 23. *The Lord is my shepherd; I shall not want. He makes me to lie down in green pastures; He leads me beside the still waters (Psalm 23:1- 2 KJV).* Examine them closely and remember that God has given us everything we need; we lack nothing. He leads us to rest. There is a purpose behind the period of rest we find ourselves in—to calm us and to remove the work-related stresses we were dealing with in preparation for what's next. For me, these are the best words of the entire Psalm: *he restores my soul.* Four little words, but to me they now mean *everything.*

He returned my soul back to me, my self-confidence, my "me." It happened for me in the Pocono Mountains of eastern Pennsylvania. I went to a place I'd never been to before to serve on an interim basis as vice president of human resources for the Pocono Health System. My role was to help stabilize the function while they conducted a search. In my head I was saying, "What on earth are you doing?" But God knew. My confidence came back. I was facing issues and situations that needed the gifts God had given me. With each new success a little confidence returned, that belief that "I can do this." God also surrounded me with some of the best people I've ever had the privilege to work with; I was part of a leadership team that truly functioned as a team. Even though I was far from home and the family I loved, I felt God's arms wrapped around me.

When I returned home six and a half months later, my soul had been restored. I left there truly feeling like a blessed man. I thought of these words from the psalm: *Surely goodness and love will follow me all the days of my life ...*

It will happen for you, too. I don't know what it will be for your soul, but you'll know when it happens. When it does, remember the 23rd Psalm.

APPENDIX

THE KUBLER-ROSS CHANGE CURVE

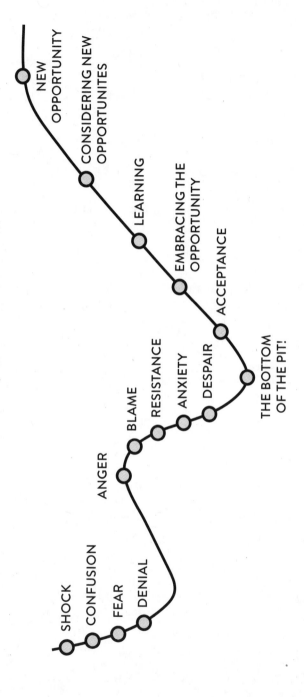

THE CHANGE CURVE

THE *KUBLER-ROSS CHANGE CURVE* is a model used to help understand the different stages of personal transition a person will go through with any type of change, personal or organizational. Losing a job is a significant personal change in your life.

The curve itself looks like a roller coaster ride because it will be a personal roller coaster for you, full of many different emotions. Each of us responds to change a little differently. How quickly you move through the various stages of change is personal. I have found some individuals, those who really enjoy change, will move very quickly through the change process going from the old to the new. However, I find most people work through the process at a slower pace. Some, those who are very resistant to change, will stay stuck and don't move at all for a long period of time.

The change curve highlights some of the main elements of change associated with a job loss and the emotions that are experienced. As it relates to losing a job, it starts with the shock of getting that news and moves through the process until you begin something new.

APPENDIX B

TOPICAL INDEX

ANGER/LETTING GO

ANXIETY, FEAR & WORRY

RE-DIRECTION

SELF CONFIDENCE

USE OF TIME

WAITING

WHY

BOOKS WORTH READING

ABOUT LIFE

Halftime: Changing Your Game Plan from Success to Significance by Bob P. Buford and Jim Collins. This book will encourage you to pause and rethink what's next for you for work and for your life, especially for those in the middle of their career.

Finishing Well: The Adventure of Life Beyond Halftime by Bob P. Buford and Ken Blanchard. This book is especially helpful for those in the second half of their career, helping you think through "what's next." The book covers a number of people, over age 40, who are "finishing well" in life.

On Fire: The 7 Choices to Ignite a Radically Inspired Life by John O'Leary. This book provides insights from John O'Leary's childhood experience of being burned and the people who came into his life to help him through the journey. He'll inspire you to live life to the fullest.

The Go-Giver by Bob Burg and John David Mann. This book will inspire you to help others you meet in life and remember that it is through giving that we receive.

Who Moved My Cheese? by Spencer Johnson and Kenneth Blanchard. This book is a simple and timeless book about dealing with change in your life. Trust me, if you're unemployed, your "cheese has moved."

FOR YOUR JOB SEARCH

People Hire People – Not Resumes by Frank V. Danzo. This book is about the job search process and provides some wonderful assistance in steps you need to take in organizing and managing your search.

Networking Is a Contact Sport by Joe Sweeney. This book will help you understand the importance of relationship building throughout your career and life.

Rites of Passage at $100,000 to $1,000,000+ by John Lucht. This book is about the executive search process, filled with tips that are practical for any job searcher.

Million Dollar Consulting: The Professional's Guide to Growing a Practice by Alan Weiss. This book is helpful for those considering starting their own business or consulting practice.

SAMPLE COMMUNICATIONS

ANNOUNCEMENTS USED WHEN I BECAME UNEMPLOYED

Following are the two announcements I used to let people know that I was unemployed. One went to family and friends, the other to those I had a work-related relationship.

FAMILY AND FRIENDS

Friends & Family

I want you to be aware that today Lutheran Senior Services announced an organizational re-structuring and my position as Vice President for Human Resources has been eliminated. Due to a pre-planned trip at the end of the week (yes, it is a golf trip), my final day with LSS will be Wednesday, October 11th. It has been a joy and blessing to serve at LSS for almost 10 years.

At this moment in time, I have mixed emotions. When you get news like this that wasn't part of your plans for the future, it really hurts and there is some natural anxiety at not being able to see into the future. But I believe Romans 8:28: "And we know that in **all things** God works for the good of those who love him, who have been called according to his purpose". This gets me really excited, focusing my energy on finding out what plans

God has in store for me next. He knows, but I don't. I also know that He is an amazing God who can do more than we can ever imagine (Ephesians 3:20).

The next item is a minor one. I've updated my e-mail address. Please update my contact information to:

Dale Kreienkamp
E-mail:
Cell: 314-xxx-xxxx

My final request is that you keep me in your prayers as I go through his journey. Thanks for your support.

Dale

WORK-RELATED RELATIONSHIPS

I want you to be aware that today Lutheran Senior Services announced an organizational re-structuring and my position as Vice President for Human Resources has been eliminated. Due to a pre-planned trip (golf) at the end of the week, my final day with LSS will be Wednesday, October 11th.

I would like to stay connected with you. My new contact information is:

Dale Kreienkamp
E-mail:
Cell: 314-xxx-xxxx

It has been a joy and blessing to serve at LSS for almost 10 years. Now my focus is on learning what plans God has in store for me next. He is an amazing God who can do more than we can ever imagine (Ephesians 3:20) and even though this wasn't part of my plans, I also believe Romans 8:28: "And we know that in **all things** God works for the good of those who love him, who have been called according to his purpose."

I look forward to connecting again soon.

Dale

MONTHLY UPDATES ABOUT MY JOB SEARCH JOURNEY

Following are samples of my monthly updates. Each month, one went to family and friends, the other to everyone that I met with in my networking journey. The one that went to family and friends reflected my Christian faith in every update.

FAMILY AND FRIENDS

To my family and good friends:

It's now April and even though you might not think so because of the weather outside, it really is spring. How do I know? A week ago we celebrated Easter and the bursting open of the tomb. He is Risen! That's the best news we ever received. Thursday of last week was the Cardinals home opener and this week was Masters week.

A week ago, my grandson Noah (2 and a half years old) was

at our home. He was playing with some toys and talking to me when I said I needed to go get something. He said to me, "grandpa wait, you have to be patient." Out of the mouths of children we get wisdom and oh how true those words are.

On the job front, the market is starting to open up a little, but there is still nothing that I'm close on. I continue to remind myself that my job is to work the process and God will open the right job for me at the right time. So, I'm practicing patience, as much as I can these days. I'm reminded of the what the scriptures say in Isaiah 40:31, [31] *But they that* **wait** *upon the Lord shall renew their strength; they shall mount up with wings as eagles; they shall run, and not be weary; and they shall walk, and not faint.* I'm waiting and getting ready to soar!

My weeks continue to be filled with networking meetings and am blessed people are opening their doors to meet with me. Those people also have been introducing me to others, which is helpful to me by expanding my network. I truly enjoy meeting with people and having these conversations. If there is someone you think would be good for me to meet with, please introduce me.

Thanks for your prayers on my behalf, they are greatly appreciated.

Dale

TO THOSE I'VE MET WITH IN MY NETWORKING JOURNEY

The page on the calendar has turned to April and my journey searching for a new career opportunity continues.

My schedule of networking has been active. I appreciate that you opened your schedule to meet with me and am thankful for the many introductions that have been made on my behalf. I continue to enjoy meeting new people, so if you have thought of someone else that would be good for me to meet with, please introduce me.

On the home front, a week ago, my grandson Noah (2 and a half years old) was at our home. He was playing with some toys and talking to me when I said I needed to go get something. He said to me, "grandpa wait, you have to be patient." Out of the mouths of children we get wisdom and oh how true those words are. This search process requires plenty of patience. I remain optimistic that the right opportunity is "right around the corner."

Thanks for your support!

Dale

INTERVIEW PREPARATION

THE INTERVIEW IS YOUR opportunity to make a good impression and highlight your special job skills. While you don't control the questions you will be asked, you can prepare yourself for the interview in advance.

1. **Self-analysis:** Take stock of the gifts that God has given to you. List what you do well, things that other people have always said are special about you—e.g., you are easy talk to, you are a great problem solver, etc.

2. **Questions about your resume:** Review your resume and think of questions you might be asked. If you have listed decreasing costs by 25% as a success, can you answer a question about how much that was in dollars? Or how did you do that? Put yourself in the shoes of the person interviewing you, what would you ask of yourself?

3. **Anticipate common questions:** There are some very common questions you can anticipate, such as, "Why do you want this job," "Tell me about yourself," "What are your strengths and weaknesses," etc. If you aren't sure what might be asked, you can go online to pull up a list of common interview questions to give you an idea.

4. **Anticipate "behavioral" questions:** Expect "behavioral" questions in an interview—e.g., being asked to give examples from your past that demonstrate your answer to certain questions. Think about your past successes as you prepare for these types of questions.

5. **Your questions of them:** Be ready with some questions to ask them—and not just about the starting rate of pay or their benefits package. Ask about what's important to you. As an example, if clarity of expectations is important to you, what question would you ask to learn more about that?

Let me be clear—you don't want to be a robot and have everything scripted out and memorized. If you do, that will be clear to the person interviewing you. What you want to do is reduce the surprises so that your natural self is what they see.

PREPARING FOR *YOUR* INTERVIEW

WHEN YOU ARE CONTACTED, and an interview is scheduled, then it's time to prepare for the interview for that job, with that organization. What's different from general interview preparation is that you know the job you are interviewing for and you know the organization. What do you do next to prepare?

1. **Company research:** Do some research about the company. You can find a wealth of information online, but you can also gather information by searching out people you know who work for them. If you know about the company, it will be clear to the interviewer that you are interested.

2. **Your questions:** Refine the list of questions you have based upon the job and the organization. Your questions will demonstrate your interest and help you determine if this is the right job for you.

3. **Your best foot forward:** Putting your best foot forward means presenting the real you. But first, you need to dress appropriately; first impressions count. If you aren't certain what the standard of dress is at the company, call and ask or ask the person who sets up the appointment. You'll never be wrong in overdressing. Remember to

smile when you meet people, even if you're nervous. A smile conveys friendliness and warmth, something all interviewers want to see.

4. **Practice answering questions:** Have your spouse or a good friend ask questions you think you might be asked and *answer them out loud.* Why? Because your mind knows what it wants to say, but it might not come out of your mouth the same way. A little practice will calm you down.

5. **Pray:** You've done all you can to prepare; it's time to turn it over to God. In my turning it over to God, I often reread Ephesians 6:13-18, especially the words I've bolded. *Therefore put on the full armor of God, so that when the day of evil comes, you may be able to stand your ground, and **after you have done everything, to stand. Stand firm then,** with the belt of truth buckled around your waist, with the breastplate of righteousness in place, and with your feet fitted with the readiness that comes from the gospel of peace. In addition to all this, take up the shield of faith, with which you can extinguish all the flaming arrows of the evil one. Take the helmet of salvation and the sword of the Spirit, which is the word of God. And pray in the Spirit on all occasions with all kinds of prayers and requests.*